Empath

———— ❦❧❦❧ ————

*2 Manuscripts Mental Toughness
and Cognitive Behavioral Therapy*

Chris S Jennings

express written consent from the Publisher. All additional right reserved.

The information in the following pages is broadly considered to be a truthful and accurate account of facts and as such any inattention, use or misuse of the information in question by the reader will render any resulting actions solely under their purview. There are no scenarios in which the publisher or the original author of this work can be in any fashion deemed liable for any hardship or damages that may befall them after undertaking information described herein.

Additionally, the information in the following pages is intended only for informational purposes and should thus be thought of as universal. As befitting its nature, it is presented without assurance regarding its prolonged validity or interim quality. Trademarks that are mentioned are done without written consent and can in no way be considered an endorsement from the trademark holder.

Table of Contents

Mental Toughness

_How to Build Mental Toughness
and Develop an Unbeatable Mind_

Chris S Jennings

Table of Contents

Introduction

Mental toughness is the ability to keep going, even if situations in life are trying to drag you down. Life is not always easy, and unfortunately, sometimes we all must deal with relationship problems, stressful, dead-end jobs, or money problems. If you have ever dealt with these types of issues, you might have felt stuck in your situation, unable to see a way out. You might have felt like you would be in the situation forever. If you have ever felt like this, you know it can feel nearly impossible to make a change in your life when you are dealing with that overwhelming "stuck" feeling. That feeling can be very defeating, and it is these situations that either require us to summon our mental toughness and turn our lives around for the better or remain in the situation and feel increasingly more defeated.

Everyone is going to experience hardships throughout their lives, but it is how we deal with these hardships that can really make or break us. Summoning your mental toughness, developing the characteristics of a mentally tough person, and improving your emotional intelligence are all ways in which you can improve your mental toughness, and in turn, your life.

A mentally tough person uses certain psychological factors and tricks to change their mindset, hence improving their entire life around for the better. By setting boundaries, practicing good communication skills, maintaining a schedule, and employing certain methods used by professional athletic coaches, as well as military leaders, you can change your life for the better and eliminate fear and anxiety in your life once and for all.

You will be able to use setbacks you encounter as opportunities, a springboard so to speak, that creates a jumping off point for you to evaluate your life and embrace the changes and challenges you encounter as a growing point, instead of as a negative setback. And finally, you will be able to reign in your anger, re-focusing it for a better purpose and using the energy you experience from the anger as a method to achieve great things.

Chapter 1:
Mentally Tough People

Characteristics of Mentally Tough People

Mental toughness is something that everyone can develop, but it does seem as if it comes more easily to some people. Have you ever noticed that some people can face conflicts head-on, sail through adverse situations, and come out better for it in the end? Anyone who can embrace a challenging situation with arms wide open probably has a great level of mental toughness, and you too can acquire this mentality. Most mentally tough people have similar personality characteristics, and these characteristics can all be developed with a little patience and practice. The good news is, if you're reading this book, you already know that you want to make a change in your life, and recognizing the need to make a change is the first and most important step. You too can develop the following characteristics to improve your mental toughness.

Confidence: Confidence is a huge factor in mental toughness. Confident people can remain resilient to change, because they know they will come out okay in the end, regardless of what happens. Your mental state plays a big role in whether you succeed or fail. Confident people are more assertive and can take charge of their situation to make the needed changes, hence developing an outcome that works out in their favor. For example, someone who lacks self-confidence might falter when making a decision, changing their mind several times or maybe even avoid making a decision in the first place. A confident person will make a decision and stick with it, knowing that they can use obstacles as an opportunity for growth. Confident people charge ahead, making decisions to get things accomplished. They envision an outcome and work toward it. They know that Henry Ford was right when he said, "Whether you think you can, or think you can't, you're right."

Ability to Welcome Change and Remain Flexible

A mentally tough person can welcome change and roll with the punches, no matter if the change is big or small. Change is not always a bad thing, and often if there is no change in your life, you are not growing as a person. Life is about learning and trying new things, and remaining in the same situation does not allow for growth or improvement in your life. A mentally tough person will embrace a challenge and adapt to change, often viewing the change, no matter how big or small, as a chance to develop a new skill or experience a new opportunity. The old saying is, "When one door closes, another opens," and sometimes a forced change is all we need to get us out of the stagnant place in which we are stuck. For example, in today's economy, jobs and businesses are constantly changing and restructuring. When companies downsize or restructure, employees are faced with job loss, and this can sometimes be devastating. A mentally strong person will seize the opportunity to improve their life by weighing all of their options. If a mentally strong person who had been considering a career change is suddenly faced with losing their job, he or she will take this time to develop their skill set, return to school, or polish their resume to make a career change. Maybe the mentally strong person had been considering starting their own business but didn't have the time or the knowledge to make it happen. This person will view their sudden abundance of extra time as a chance to grow and develop as a person, starting their business and making things happen, instead of lounging in front of the television, crying relentlessly about their situation.

Refuse to Let Fear Hold Them Back

A mentally tough person does not let fear hold them back. Everyone must go through challenges in life, and it is how we view those challenges that can shape our lives for the better. Change is scary, but so is remaining in the same stagnant situation indefinitely. Moving to a new city, completely changing careers, or leaving a relationship can be scary, but the reality is, you are considering this change for a reason. Maybe you're unhappy with the job opportunities in your small town, maybe there is no room for growth in your current career, or maybe you and your partner have some differences that cannot be resolved with a compromise. Whatever the situation is, a mentally strong person does not let fear of the unknown hold them back. Think about the area in your life in which you want to make a change. Now think about how you would feel if you are in this exact same situation in a year, two years, or even five years from now. Will you be even more miserable? Even though change can be terrifying, it is often even more terrifying to remain stuck in the same situation indefinitely, all because you fear the unknown. A mentally tough person would rather be scared for a short amount of time while they are going through a change in life than live in fear of the change, never improving or bettering their situation.

Will Not Let Toxic People Affect Them

A toxic person is someone who ruins the environment or the atmosphere for those around them. The toxic person might be incredibly jealous, judgmental, or just negative overall. A toxic person is like the grown-up version of the playground bully: he or she has low self-esteem and is so unhappy with their own lives, so they are constantly trying to bring others down to their level. The toxic person might discredit all of your ideas or find something that can go wrong in every situation. The toxic person is usually projecting their own insecurities onto you, sometimes unknowingly. The toxic person is not a mentally healthy person and can quickly drag others down. Someone who is mentally strong will avoid this type of person in general, or at the very least, not let the toxic person's opinions bother them. In some situations, it is impossible to avoid toxic people. If there is a toxic person in your workplace, odds are you can't avoid this person at all times. A mentally strong person realizes this and will do their best to see things from the toxic person's point of view if possible. A mentally strong person also realizes that the toxic person is unhappy, so he or she will not let the toxic opinions and attitude affect them and their work. Although the mentally strong person might not agree with the toxic person's opinion, the mentally strong person will listen to the toxic person's opinion and does not engage in an argument. The mentally strong person has the knowledge and the self-esteem to treat everyone with respect, even if they do not agree with what is being said. The mentally strong person knows that the toxic person is just that, toxic, and he or she will not let this person ruin their day or the outcome of a situation.

Chapter 1: Mentally Tough People

Exert Assertiveness

A mentally strong person is assertive. They say what they mean, and they mean what they say. They know how to use concise language so that the meaning of their words is not mistaken and their intentions are not taken the wrong way. Mentally strong people know how to say no. They know that it's ok to take time to themselves, whether that means saying no to an invitation they don't want to accept or simply staying in on a Saturday night to recharge. Mentally strong people also know when to set boundaries. For example, if someone asks them a personal question and they don't want to answer the question, the mentally strong person will have no problem saying that they are uncomfortable answering the question. A mentally strong person can stick up for themselves and does not let other people take advantage of them.

The Difference Between Being Mentally Strong and Acting Tough

A person who is "acting tough" is most likely someone who in reality is not mentally strong. The tough person uses intimidation tactics to fake their own mental strength. They might bully other people by taking control of a situation, or they might simply demand that things go their way, never willing to compromise or listen to anyone else's opinion. If you are working on a project that requires everyone to collaborate and discuss solutions for a mutually agreeable outcome, yet there is one person who insists that everything goes his or her way, that person is probably just acting tough and in all actuality, is insecure. As previously discussed, a mentally strong person can remain flexible in most situations, embraces change and welcomes challenges, and can put themselves in someone else's shoes to better understand another viewpoint. Tough people live to feel powerful, and to a tough person, being in charge, running the show, and bossing people around makes them feel powerful. Although this toughness may make someone seem invincible at first glance, the tough-acting person only sees one way in which to solve a problem: their way. If their way does not work to solve said problem or complete a task, the tough-acting person will be devastated. A tough-acting person does not embrace change or view failure as a chance to develop because they do not have the ability to see how their perceived failure can help them grow. The tough-acting person only sees one thing: failure. Their ego is damaged, and they are unable to embrace the challenge to learn the lesson of how things can be improved for next time. A mentally strong person knows there is more than one way to solve a problem. He or she not only welcomes other people's viewpoints but will use a failure as a chance to grow and develop, constantly improving themselves as a person. They will take other opinions into consideration and try to see things from all angles.

How Emotional Intelligence Affects the Ability to be Mentally Strong

Emotional intelligence is the ability to understand and demonstrate emotions in a mature, acceptable manner. Someone who is emotionally intelligent can recognize and classify the feelings that he or she is experiencing at any given time. An emotionally intelligent person can also recognize why they are feeling their emotions and make appropriate changes in their life to feel their intended emotions. For example, if an emotionally intelligent person encounters someone who is rude to them, the emotionally intelligent person can recognize that they are feeling offended because a rude comment was made, and then will remove themselves from the company of the rude person. The emotionally intelligent person also can recognize that it is the rude person who is in the wrong, and not themselves. Furthermore, the emotionally intelligent person will not take the "bait" for an argument, yelling back or letting the rude person antagonize them. They will simply set boundaries and move on, recognizing that the other person was in the wrong.

Although emotional intelligence and mental strength go hand in hand, they are not quite the same thing. Emotional intelligence is a key component of mental strength. As previously discussed, the mentally strong person will embrace challenges, can put themselves in others' shoes, and can distance themselves from toxic people. It takes emotional intelligence to recognize when someone else is in the wrong. A mentally strong person can adapt to change, distance themselves from toxic people, exert confidence and assertiveness, and not let fear hold them back. It takes emotional intelligence to recognize all of these situations and to process the feelings and actions that go along with these circumstances in an appropriate manner.

Chapter 2:
Seven Steps for Improving
Your Emotional Intelligence

Emotional intelligence is paramount to living a happy, healthy life. It may seem like some people are born with confidence, or that some people are predisposed to a high level of emotional intelligence, and depending on the environment in which someone grew up, their background and life experiences, emotional intelligence may come easier to some people than it does to others. Some people need to work much harder than others to get and maintain a healthy level of emotional intelligence. Luckily, there are ways to improve your emotional intelligence, and all it takes is a little practice and some self-awareness. Emotional intelligence can be improved upon in many ways, but here are seven methods that you should make a habit of practicing.

Believe Your Intuition

Intuition is that little gut feeling you have, that nagging in the back of your mind, when you are trying to make a decision or decide whether or not to trust a situation. Our gut feelings or intuition are often based on past experiences in similar situations. Your gut is telling you something for a reason, and more often than not it tends to be correct. While some people dismiss this feeling, intuitive people listen to what their mind is trying to tell them. If you have ever had to make a decision and were leaning heavily towards one outcome, or if you've ever been in a situation where your stomach was upset, and you felt nervous, that was your intuition trying to tell you something. There are countless stories of people who have done something that proved to be beneficial in the end, yet couldn't explain why they acted the way they did at the time. Perhaps someone impulsively decided to take a different route to work, but couldn't decide what made them decide to take an outer road instead of the highway, only to find out later that they made the right decision because there was a major accident on their usual route to work. Not only did the intuitive person avoid sitting in traffic, but he or she may also have prevented themselves from being involved in a serious or fatal accident. Unexplained decisions or events such as these are your intuition at work.

Intuition is a sign of emotional intelligence. You can improve your intuition by taking the time to spend alone, concentrating on your thoughts, journaling, and paying attention to what your mind is trying to tell you. The mind is a powerful thing, if only we let it work to its full capacity. The more you pay attention to your thoughts, the stronger your intuition will become.

Set Boundaries

Any relationship, whether it's a romantic relationship, a relationship between co-workers, a friendship, or a family relationship, should have healthy boundaries. An emotionally intelligent person recognizes their own feelings and can determine if someone else's inappropriate words or actions are causing them to feel uncomfortable. An emotionally intelligent person knows what they are willing to put up with, and what behaviors are intolerable. An emotionally intelligent person is direct and will tell someone if their language or behavior is making them uncomfortable because they can recognize their own feelings and are in tune with why they feel the way they do. The emotionally intelligent person is also able to set boundaries and be assertive because they do not allow themselves to feel guilty for feeling a certain way.

An emotionally intelligent person knows what their values are and will not compromise these values. If someone does something to go against what the emotionally intelligent person believes, there will be consequences in place for the behavior. For example, if a friend continues to cancel plans or does not show up when the plans are made, the emotionally intelligent person would recognize that the friend has crossed a boundary, and he or she must decide if the consequence they wish to bestow upon the offending friend is to end the friendship. If someone continues to treat someone else badly, but the recipient of the bad behavior continues to allow it to happen, the offender is receiving no consequences, and will, therefore, continue to upset the other person with their undesirable behavior. The offender is taking advantage of the other person, who is unwilling or has not chosen to set boundaries. An emotionally intelligent person will let the other person know that his or her behavior is not acceptable. Quite possibly, the offender may not have even known their actions were upsetting to the other person. If the upsetting actions continue, then the offender clearly does not respect the other person's boundaries, and consequences should be enforced, whether that means ending the friendship or keeping the other person at a distance. The emotionally intelligent person has no problem setting boundaries and enforcing these boundaries because they have the self-confidence to know that they are worth receiving fair treatment.

Practice Good Communication

An emotionally intelligent person has excellent communication skills because they know what they want, have set their boundaries, and do not waste time mincing words or saying things that can be construed in a way other than they intended. They also practice good communication skills by listening when speaking to someone. When conversing with someone, the emotionally intelligent person listens to what the other person is saying. They make eye contact and don't become distracted by their phone or other people around them. They listen to hear what is being said, they don't just listen to see how they can respond with their own story. People like to feel appreciated, and anyone who is taking the time to talk to you does not want to be outdone by your story or made to feel like you couldn't wait for their story to end so you could share your own story. The emotionally intelligent person also thinks before he or she speaks. If you have only listened to someone else talk so that you could have your own turn, you have not allowed yourself the time to process what they are saying and respond appropriately. The emotionally intelligent person does not just blurt out the first thing that comes to mind; they reflect on what the speaker said and respond appropriately.

Another important aspect of good communication is body language. Emotionally intelligent people are in tune not only with themselves but with those around them. Making eye contact, smiling, and keeping your body turned towards the speaker are all signs of good communication skills. Folding your arms, shuffling impatiently back and forth, turning your body away from the speaker, and constantly checking your phone are sure signs that you are not paying attention to what the speaker is saying. Not only is this behavior rude, but it does not lend itself to good communication because you are not devoting your full attention to the speaker, which may cause you to miss some key points.

Just as in-person communication skills are vital to a good conversation, an emotionally intelligent person knows that written communication is just as important. Double check text messages and emails to make sure they say exactly what you intend to say. Remember, mentally tough and emotionally intelligent people will be direct with their words so that the intended meaning of their message cannot be misconstrued. Check for typos or words that have been corrected to mean something else. Read the text message or email out loud to yourself if you are unsure of how it sounds. Taking a few extra seconds to double check your work is worth the embarrassment of inadvertently sending the wrong message.

Overcome Obstacles in Life

An emotionally intelligent person can overcome obstacles in their life. They view obstacles as a challenge and often have a game plan and a backup plan in case their original plan does not work. The first step to overcoming an obstacle is to break the process down into smaller, more manageable chunks. It is impossible to write an entire novel in a day, so maybe the emotionally intelligent person will make it their goal to write one chapter a week. Likewise, an emotionally intelligent person who has just lost their job might make it their goal to apply to three jobs per day, taking the time to perfect their cover letter and tailor their resume to each of these jobs. An emotionally intelligent person will then chart their progress and reflect back on their journey. Perhaps he or she will note on a calendar what jobs they applied for on what day, or maybe they will reflect on how they can manage their time more wisely to write two chapters of their novel in a week instead of only one chapter.

In addition to setting small goals, an emotionally intelligent person is not afraid to ask for guidance and input, or a listening ear at the very least. An emotionally intelligent person embraces challenges and obstacles but also welcomes opinions from other sources. He or she knows it sometimes pays to get other perspectives on a situation, and someone else could bring a new outlook that he or she hadn't thought of. A true emotionally intelligent person welcomes other perspectives, while someone who is only acting tough wants to do things their own way all the time.

One quick way to overcome an obstacle or get a new perspective is to simply take a break. Go outside, get some fresh air, take the dog for a walk. Giving your mind a break and a chance to think about something else will give you a fresh look when you go back to said obstacle. Upon your return, you can evaluate the obstacle. Is this as difficult as it once seemed? A change of scenery could very well change your entire approach.

Maintain a Schedule

An emotionally intelligent person knows there is a benefit to maintain a daily routine. While in our younger days we might have balked at the idea of getting up early and living by a set schedule, an emotionally intelligent person knows a schedule is vital to reducing stress. Imagine if you woke up late every day with no plan for the day. It might sound fun at first, but the truth is, most people would become depressed sitting around all day with nothing to do, or on the opposite end of the spectrum, they would become stressed out by the number of tasks they need to complete without any rhyme or reason of when these tasks needed to be completed.

If you make a list of all the things you need to accomplish for the day, then cross them off individually when you complete each task, you will be amazed at the sense of accomplishment you feel. Seeing your progress as you make your way down the list not only makes you feel productive, it actually *is* productive. Moving from one task to the next gives you an end goal in sight, and you can see the award of free time, the proverbial light shining at the end of the tunnel.

Chapter 2: Seven Steps for Improving Your Emotional Intelligence

Not only does this routine give you a feeling of accomplishment, but it helps you eliminate wasted time, much of which is most likely spent making nonessential decisions. For example, if you get into the habit of going to the gym first thing in the morning, you won't have to spend the rest of your day trying to decide when and if you should go; you will already be done for the day.

A mentally strong person thrives on the daily routine because it provides a sense of accomplishment, which also boosts confidence and self-esteem. They can see the progress they have made each day, which in turn motivates the mentally strong person to persevere.

Eliminate Fear of Rejection

Rejection, or even the fear of rejection, can be very painful, but emotionally intelligent people know that sometimes rejection is just a part of life, and they view rejections as one more opportunity for self-improvement and a chance to grow. By practicing a few techniques and improving self-esteem, you can eliminate the fear of rejection. The first step to eliminating this fear is to stop assuming you will be rejected in the first place. When people assume they will be rejected, they subconsciously display behaviors that ultimately get them rejected. The fear of rejection ultimately becomes a reality.

Another way to eliminate the fear of rejection is to picture yourself succeeding. The mind is a powerful thing, and if you think positively, not allowing yourself to picture or see yourself in a rejected state, you can overcome this fear.

A final solution to overcoming the fear of rejection is to give yourself options so that if one thing doesn't work out, you will have other possibilities. Rejection from one job interview does not feel as defeating if you have already lined up other interviews, or at the very least, if you have applied at other places of employment. If you are applying for a job, odds are in today's economy, the company is receiving hundreds, possibly thousands, of applications to fill only one position. It goes without saying that the company will not be able to hire every single person. By applying for several jobs at once, or even branching out to consider a different, yet similar line of work, you are opening up more possibilities for yourself and reducing your fear of rejection.

An emotionally healthy person can keep their mind open to new possibilities and different opportunities, even if the new situation is out of their comfort zone. An emotionally healthy person steps out of their comfort zone, accepts new challenges, and gives themselves plenty of options, so they do not have to feel rejected by just one person or opportunity.

Reduce Anxiety

An emotionally intelligent person understands that feeling anxious is not beneficial. It is normal to be nervous before a test, a job interview, or a huge presentation, but when the panicky feelings, upset stomach, rapid heartbeat, and sweaty palms become an everyday occurrence, anxiety is taking its toll on your body and preventing you from achieving your goals. If you let it go on too long, anxiety can snowball and negatively affect your life.

Part of being an emotionally intelligent person is recognizing your feelings and identifying what is causing them. Realizing that you are feeling anxious is the first step. Once you can accept the fact that you are feeling anxious and that it's okay to feel this way, you can identify the source of the anxiety. Begin by asking yourself whether or not your fears are real, if the situation or scenario you are imagining is likely to happen, and, worse-case scenario, if it does happen, will it really matter tomorrow, next week, next month, etc.

One way to eliminate anxiety is to focus your attention somewhere else. Take a break from what is bothering you and cross a few tasks off of that to-do list you made earlier. By accomplishing a goal you already set for yourself, you will experience a sense of accomplishment and improved self-esteem, which are key factors in emotional intelligence.

Chapter 3:
Learn Psychological Factors That Help You View Setbacks as Opportunities

Enhance Performance by Transferring Negative Energy Generated by Nervousness into Shatterproof Confidence

Nervousness can come in a variety of ways. It is normal to feel nervous before a job interview or a presentation at work. When the event that is causing you to feel nervous is over, you no longer feel nervous because there is nothing to be nervous about the task is complete and you cannot change the outcome. The job interview is over, and you will eventually receive a phone call or email to let you know whether or not you got the job. The presentation at work is over, and either everyone loved it, and they will be buying your product, or the entire audience played on their phones the entire time and didn't even pay attention to your presentation. At any rate, the nerve-wracking situation is over, and you don't have to feel nervous anymore. Everyone has experienced nervous energy in some way, shape, or form. When you have nervous energy, you feel as if you could complete everything on your To Do list at once, you have the energy to burn, or you talk fast and can't sit still. You might be jittery, tapping a pen on your desk or crossing, uncrossing, then re-crossing your legs and shaking your foot. It is completely normal to feel nervous before a big event that is out of your everyday routine. Veteran teachers get nervous before the first day of school, and even brain surgeons get nervous before they perform a surgery. Having that nervous feeling is normal and proves that you care about the event that is happening. If you never felt nervous before you accomplished anything out of the ordinary, it would appear as if you didn't care about the situation at hand.

It is how we deal with the nervous energy that can often change the outcome of the event. For example, if you show up to a job interview and your hands are shaking, your voice is cracking, and you fidget in your chair the entire time, this will not make a good first impression on the interviewer(s). Even though they know you are nervous, they will more than likely go with another candidate who did not appear as nervous as you did, even though he or she could have been just as nervous, or maybe even more nervous than you were. It's a cruel world we live in, but if you use the tips found in this book, you can change your nervous energy into shatterproof confidence and win people over every time.

Analyze Your Fears: The first thing you should do when you begin to feel this nervous energy is to analyze your fears. What is making you feel this way? Are you truly this nervous about the job interview itself, or are there more feelings attached to your nerves? Are you afraid that you will feel like a failure if you don't get the job? Are you afraid that your family, friends, or spouse will think you are a failure if you don't get the job? Are your fears rational? Sometimes it can be so easy to overthink or overanalyze our thoughts, and before we know it, we have created an entire scenario in our heads that would almost never happen in real life. Take a look at what is making you nervous and first determine if what you are fearing is something that could be a potential outcome of the situation. If your fear is rational, keep reading to determine how to change these nerves to positive energy.

Remember the Positive Side

There is a positive side to feeling these nerves-you are alive and feeling! Although it can be tricky, you must train your brain to see the good in every situation. Embrace the challenge that life is giving you and learn to improve from it. For example, a job interview is a chance for both parties to learn about each other. This is your chance to see if you would actually like to work for this company. Do you fit in with their employees? Does the company operate with the same set of standards and values that you hold to be true? Odds are, the hiring committee has received a plethora of applications, and many of these applications did not even get a second glance or a call for an interview. You have made it to the job interview, which is more than many of the applicants can say! An emotionally intelligent person will use this nervous opportunity as a way to learn and grow. They will view the nerve-wracking event as a challenge.

Chapter 3: Learn Psychological Factors That Help You View Setbacks as Opportunities

The next time you have to go through the same or similar situation, you will be wiser and more experienced, using the previous challenges upon which to grow and build.

What is the Worst That Can Happen?

One way to calm your nerves is to further analyze the situation by asking yourself what the worst possible outcome could be. If the situation you are so nervous about does not end up with an outcome that you find favorable, what is the worst that can happen as a result? What if you don't get the interview or the clients do not buy your product, or you mess up your speech? Although these would all be disappointing, you can still go on more interviews, maybe for an even better job opportunity. You can pitch your product to more clients, maybe even to clients who would buy a larger quantity of your product or who would refer you to other businesses. You can use the speech you gave as an opportunity to practice, and next time maybe you will rehearse more before you go in front of a huge audience. At any rate, one major key to transferring this nervous energy into shatterproof confidence is to ask yourself, "What is the worst that can happen?" At the very least, you are getting more experience, opening yourself up to new challenges, and improving your emotional intelligence by using this nerve-wracking experience as an opportunity for growth. As an emotionally intelligent human being, you are recognizing your feelings and analyzing what is causing them, which will only improve your emotional intelligence, self-awareness, and self-confidence

Tell Yourself You Are Excited

One surefire way to use your anxious state to fuel a successful outcome is to tell yourself that you are actually excited instead of nervous. You can "trick" your brain into thinking that the nervous feelings and symptoms you feel are due to excitement instead of nerves, as the adrenaline-rush feeling of excitement is very similar to a nervous feeling. In both situations your heart is beating fast, your hands are sweaty, and you feel a jittery energy. Think, for instance, how you feel on a rollercoaster ride. The adrenaline rush and the thrill as the cart jerks around the corner and drops you straight down the track can be heart-thumping. Your body experiences the same symptoms when you are nervous. By telling yourself that you are excited about this new opportunity or situation, your brain will have a different response, using the nervous feelings for good instead of trying to dispel the symptoms, which can sometimes actually make them worse.

Learn About the Situation

Nerves and the nervous feeling you get from certain situations are often based on the unknown. In reality, there is no way to predict the outcome of every situation. We frequently become nervous when we don't know what will happen or what something will entail. One way to calm your nerves and become more confident is to learn about the situation. Take some time to do some research, ask a friend or colleague, or do some online searching. Most people are more than willing to share their experiences and offer advice, if only they are asked. You would be surprised at the amount of people who have already been in your situation, or who can point you in the right direction of someone who can help. If you are going to a job interview, research the company before you go. Go online to do a Google search on interview tips. Ask a trusted friend or colleague for tips on how they present themselves in an interview, or for key points on how to dress if you are unsure. Just knowing that someone else is in your corner and that you are not alone can make all the difference in transferring your nervous energy into confidence.

Keep a Journal

Keeping a journal is a tried and true method that helps reduce stress and anxiety and can help focus that nervous energy on a positive mission. When you keep a journal, you are doing something creative, which benefits the brain. Writing about events in your life, even if you only write for a few minutes a day, provides a release for your emotions. It has been proven that putting pen to paper and allowing your brain to flow naturally is good for improving creativity and reducing stress. When you write, your brain is connected to your hand, and your hand flows freely, letting your mind go. Keeping a journal and writing things down can help you process your thoughts. Writing things down is a good way to keep track of daily events and allows you to go back and reflect on your experiences and thoughts. You might be amazed at the progress you see in just a short amount of time, and once this progress is recorded on paper, you can see the changes and improvements right in front of your eyes. Journaling also allows you to brainstorm, coming up with new ideas and outlooks on things. You might think your life is not worth writing about, but once you begin to write, letting the creative juices flow, new ideas will emerge, and you will develop a new outlook on things. In addition to tracking your daily events, you can also use your journal to write about how you reacted to these events. By writing about your emotions, you are getting them out of your head and not allowing them to stay pent up inside. You can look back at the progress you have made, both emotionally and in the way you overcome obstacles. You can celebrate your successes and track your progress. Getting your feelings down on paper allows you to process that nervous energy and reflect on what is causing it. By reflecting on your feelings and understanding what your brain is thinking, you are improving your emotional intelligence, and using that energy for good.

Spend Time with Friends or Loved Ones

Humans are pack animals by nature, and human interaction is key to a happy, fulfilling life. It is nice to feel loved, and spending time with old friends, sharing inside jokes and telling stories is a major confidence booster. Our friends and families understand us and have been with us through thick and thin. When spending time with close friends and family, we often feel that we don't have to put on a façade; we can simply be ourselves. Spending time with those who appreciate us automatically gives us a great feeling and a boost of confidence. We all have that one friend or family member who can make any experience a good time. Time spent with this person is full of non-stop laughter, and you often find you are in a much better mood after you leave their company. As it turns out, laughter has several health benefits, including stress-relief. Laughing, especially that deep belly-laugh has been proven to improve circulation, reduce stress, and give you an overall relaxed feeling. Laughter also releases endorphins and serotonin, which are chemicals in the brain associated with happiness and satisfaction. Those people who laugh regularly also have healthier immune systems and make better life choices. Happy, laughing people tend to attract other healthy, laughing people. Laughter brings people closer together, and we tend to see our friends and family more frequently when we feel close to them. When you surround yourself with like people, you feel valued and appreciated, and your confidence is boosted.

Learn a New Task or Skill

If you are feeling nervous, another good way to harness that energy and build your self-confidence is by learning a new task or skill. Occupying your mind and forcing yourself to focus on something other than what is bothering you is a great way to reduce some of that nervous energy and improve your self-confidence. If there is a hobby you have always been interested in but never learned how to do, now is the time to focus your energy in that direction. Keeping your mind occupied and removing yourself from the situation of whatever is making you nervous is a great way to get over these feelings. By removing yourself from the situation, you will be able to return later with a fresh perspective, and learning something new is a great way to focus your energy. By practicing a new craft, watching a YouTube video to learn how to do something, or simply reading up on a new subject, you are occupying your mind and switching gears. Not only will this newfound knowledge be beneficial in your life, but you will feel a sense of accomplishment knowing that you have learned something new. Crossing things off your bucket list is the ultimate confidence-booster. Improving your confidence, becoming knowledgeable about a new hobby or skill, and then being able to share your newfound knowledge with others is a great way to harness and refocus your energy, giving you an ultimate rise in confidence and satisfaction.

Eliminate Unwanted Activities or Duties

In this day and age, it becomes extremely easy to overbook our schedules and overcommit to things that we deem priorities. Before you know it, you have something planned for every evening of the week and you are left with none of the much-needed alone time that is valuable in decompressing and de-stressing. Since you are overbooked this week, you are in and out of your house so quickly that the path from your front door to your kitchen counter is littered with the shoes you threw off and the junk mail you didn't open yet. By the end of the week, it becomes easy to feel exhausted, run-down, and over-extended. The clutter only adds to your level of stress and anxiety. If you are feeling overextended, take some time to consider whether or not all of these social obligations are really necessary. Yes, sometimes we all have a busy week, but there are some things we could clear from our calendar and not think twice about. Take a few minutes to analyze your social calendar and determine whether or not you are actually looking forward to each and every one of these activities. If there is an event that you are not excited about, or even worse, an event you are dreading, make the decision to rescind your RSVP.

Being assertive and setting boundaries are an integral part of emotional intelligence, and your confidence will skyrocket once you can achieve these goals and free up your schedule. Not only will your confidence surge from your ability to be assertive and set boundaries, but you will have more free time to focus on other confidence-boosting activities, such as learning a new skill, journaling, or spending time with friends and loved ones.

Do Something Nice for Someone Else

Another way to eliminate nervous energy and boost your confidence is by doing something nice for someone else. Completing a task for someone else, even if it's something small, can boost your endorphins and leave you, and the other person, elated. Performing a nice task allows you to focus your energy on something positive and keep your mind off your worries as well. When you help someone else out, whether it's by sharing your knowledge to help them solve a problem, or by completing an actual task, you are taking your mind off of your worries and focusing your energy elsewhere. Once you are finished with the task, you might have a new perspective on your original problem, or you might simply have exerted all of your energy, spending that nervous energy wisely. An additional bonus of doing something nice for someone else is that feeling of appreciation you will get from that person. When they bestow their thanks upon you, you feel appreciated and loved, and that boosts your self-confidence as well.

Chapter 3: Learn Psychological Factors That Help You View Setbacks as Opportunities

Exercise

Get rid of that nervous energy with a trip to the gym. It's a well-known fact that exercise is beneficial in many areas of your life, so next time you feel like you could run around the block with all that pen up nervous energy, it might behoove you to lace up those running shoes and do exactly that. In addition to eliminating some of that nervous energy, exercise is also a key confidence booster, but most likely in more ways than you might think. Exercise is a key component in the reduction of stress. Not only does it work off some of that energy, but it also reduces stress by boosting endorphins. Just a few short workout sessions a week can be as beneficial as taking an anti-depressant. When you are under less stress, your confidence is boosted, and you have an overall more positive outlook on life. Increased confidence comes from not only from the chemicals in your brain but also from your physical appearance as well. When you exercise your clothes fit better, and you look better, which ultimately boosts your confidence. Exercise increases blood flow, which in turn gives you a healthy glow. Exercise has also been proven to boost brain power, which can benefit and enhance self-confidence.

De-clutter

One solution that is often overlooked in the many methods of reducing nervous energy is the simple act of de-cluttering. Getting rid of junk mail, keeping everything in its place, and keeping an overall tidy home is a relatively simple way to de-stress and keep nervous energy at bay. When you are surrounded by or living in an untidy atmosphere, it can be nerve-wracking trying to find your keys each morning before work or your favorite pair of shoes to complete your outfit. If everything has its place and you know where to find things, you can eliminate the waste of time and frantic energy you spend trying to find things that you need. The more time you spend running around searching for things frantically, the more your anxiety levels rise. When you are surrounded by clutter, you feel nervous and unorganized, which can, in turn, lower your confidence. If you put yourself in a calm state, you will not force yourself to feel frenzied and out of character. Keeping a sense of calm and order in your life is paramount to boosting confidence and emotional intelligence.

Take Your Pet for a Walk

By getting outside and getting a breath of fresh air, a change of scenery, and a change in your thought process, you can reduce nervous energy and refocus your thoughts. Even a quick walk around the block with Fido can be monumental in eliminating nervous energy. Not only are you getting exercise, exerting your nervous energy for good, and increasing your blood flow, but you are taking a break from the task or thing that is causing the stress, allowing yourself to come back after your walk with a fresh outlook. You will enjoy the change of scenery, and your dog will appreciate getting out as well. Taking care of an animal who loves and depends on you is rewarding, and knowing that you are needed can boost your self-confidence as well.

Act Confident

When all else fails, act like you are confident and your brain will eventually believe itself. Acting confident is not the same as acting conceited. A mentally intelligent person knows the difference between confidence and cockiness, and he or she will display their behavior to reflect this knowledge. Keep your values and beliefs intact and remain willing to listen to other people and their suggestions. Changing your body language can have a monumental effect on your self-confidence and the way that others perceive you. By standing tall, walking with a purpose, and not crossing your arms when sitting or standing, you are tricking your brain into thinking that you are confident. Look at yourself in the mirror and recite affirmative statements in your head. By displaying these actions and hearing affirmative words, your brain will start to believe what it sees and hears, and you will feel and act with a higher level of self-confidence.

Enhance Visualization Techniques and Learn to Create Success Imagery That Will Generate Powerful Results

Picturing success is just the first step to achieving success. People who are successful in life do not let themselves picture anything but success. Creating success imagery is vital to improving self-confidence and emotional intelligence. You may have heard stories of little elderly ladies lifting cars off their grandchildren after a car accident. Although this superhuman feat of strength is attributed to the adrenaline rush in the heat of the moment, at no point in time did the person question or doubt that she could lift the car to save a life. She knew what had to be done at the moment and then reacted quickly without a second thought. Your success imagery and visualization techniques should be exactly that-no room for second guesses or doubts. You know what you want your end goal to look like, and that's the image that should remain in your head as a constant.

Before you can begin your road to success, you must picture what you want success to look like. Everyone wants to be successful, but success looks different to some people. Do you imagine that to be successful you must own a mansion, drive an expensive car, and make a six-figure salary? Or do you define success as owning your own home and working in a career you enjoy? The meaning and picture of success can be different for everyone, and that's okay. But before you can make a vague goal about wanting to be successful in life, you should first determine what you want success to look like.

The image you picture in your head might be completely different from where you are in life now, and this too is okay. You must be willing to work hard and put in the necessary steps to create your own success. This is where your mental toughness and emotional intelligence will come into play. You should picture yourself accomplishing your goal, no matter what you encounter and what obstacles you will face. Picturing success boosts confidence, and confidence is what will lead you to be successful.

Creating success imagery takes training practice. You have to train your brain to think in terms of success, especially if you are making some changes in your life from where you currently are now. Odds are if you are dreaming of success, you are not happy with where you are now in life, and that is okay too. The first step in realizing you want to achieve more success is to realize just that-that you want to achieve more success. If you already know that you want to make a change in one or more areas of your life, then you have already taken the first step.

The mind is a powerful tool, and we can use our brain and the images we produce to either help or hinder us. The images we see of ourselves often determine the reality of our situation. Many females have teetered around in high heels, paranoid about tripping and falling in front of a crowd of people. They become so obsessed with the vision of themselves tripping over their heels and falling in front of a crowd of people, and that image in their brain ultimately becomes a self-fulfilling prophecy. On the opposite end of the spectrum, athletes who use visualization techniques to create success imagery often picture themselves winning a game or competition and will ultimately win said game or competition because it becomes so ingrained in their brain that they can't imagine a scenario in which winning does not occur.

When you picture completing a task or achieving a goal in your head, your brain automatically releases the same responses it would as if you had already completed the task at hand. After you begin this practice of positive mental imagery, visualization techniques, and success imagery, you will begin to believe it yourself, and your body will respond automatically as if there is no other option for an outcome.

Picturing yourself succeeding is monumental to improving and maintaining self-esteem. Positive mental images can also reduce stress because you are picturing your success instead of worrying about failure and all the aftermath that comes with it. Use affirmative language when speaking not only to yourself but to your friends and family as well. If you have shared your goals with others, use language when speaking about your goal that does not allow for failure. Use phrases such as, "When I..." "I will..." "I can't wait to..." etc.

You have already begun part of the process- realizing that you want to change and making choices in your life to determine how you will actually make these changes. Success imagery is a powerful tool and can be used in a multitude of ways. Before you begin to make the change toward success, you should first choose a specific end goal. What do you want to accomplish? Do you want to publish a book? Earn a degree? Complete your Master's program?

Once you have your end goal in sight, break that goal into smaller, more attainable goals. If you want to write a book, determine how many paragraphs, pages, or chapters you can accomplish at any given time. Make your goal realistic so that you do not set yourself up for failure. If you know your schedule will realistically only allow you to finish a chapter a week, make that your goal. Picture in your head where you will do your writing, what time of day you will write, and the literal process of how you will accomplish this. Will you type everything out on in Microsoft Word, saving along the way, or will you write in a notebook first so that you have the creative freedom to just let your brain flow? Although these may sound like minor details, these are the types of things you must break down to set your realistic goal. The more details you can imagine, the better the process will work for you.

After you have broken down your end goal into smaller, more manageable chunks, write these smaller goals out. Make a list of everything you need to accomplish for each goal, including the time it will take to accomplish the smaller goals.

Include all five senses in your success imagery. What will it feel like to have finally accomplished your goal? Of course, you will feel like a weight has been lifted off your shoulders, but what other emotions will you feel? Happiness, pride, a sense of accomplishment, and a boost in self-confidence are imminent. When you do accomplish this goal, what sounds will you hear, what smells will you smell, what will you taste, and what will you see? If your book is published, you might smell the fresh pages of a new novel, hear the congratulatory message from your husband on the phone, taste the celebratory champagne you share with your best friend, see your book on the shelves in the bookstore, and feel the weight of the book in your hand or the pen you use to autograph a copy of your book. Picturing the entire scenario from beginning to end and every little detail will improve your confidence and will give you a positive push in the right direction.

You have already imagined how you will feel once you accomplish your own goal, but now imagine how your goal would feel through the eyes of a bystander or loved one. What would it be like for a spectator to be in the audience as you give your successful speech or book talk? What questions might they ask you and how will you respond? What would an aerial view of your success look like, or what would your success look like through the eyes of someone who was interviewing you and telling your story? Picturing your success, using visualization techniques and success imagery from every angle will give you a firm grasp on your goal and will further cement the success in your brain. With all the positive images from every angle, there is no way you can fail.

Celebrate your milestones along the way. You have an end goal in sight, but each of the smaller goals you have set is a goal that you are accomplishing as well, so it's important to give yourself credit for this as well. Celebrating your smaller achievements along the way will also boost your self-confidence, which will be even more motivation to keep moving towards the end goal.

Have a backup plan for any hurdles you might encounter. Successful, confident people know that all success does not always come without some disappointment and failure along the way. The mentally tough person views obstacles as a learning process and sees failures as an opportunity to revamp and revise their existing plan. He or she knows there will be unexpected situations that crop up along the way, and they usually have a plan to resolve these issues. Keeping the end goal and your successful images in mind, think about what hurdles you might overcome and how you can overcome these hurdles. If your goal is to write a novel and you want to write a chapter a week, think about how you can manage your time. Can you wake up thirty minutes earlier each day while your household is still quiet so that you can have some time for yourself to write? Can you leave your phone out of reach while you write so that you are not tempted to check Facebook or Instagram? Try to anticipate what roadblocks you could encounter and be proactive about fixing these issues before they become a problem.

Odds are, even if you have your end goal in mind, you have your larger goal broken down into smaller goals, and you even have a backup plan for your backup plan, you will still need to fix some problems, especially if you have a lengthy or detailed goal in mind. There is nothing wrong with revising your goal and revamping your method, or even starting completely over from scratch, as long as you don't beat yourself up over the process. Everyone makes mistakes, and these mistakes can be a jumping off point that will lead you in a whole different direction. Mentally tough people know that they can change their plan and still be successful in the end. Mentally tough people keep their success image in sight and their end goal in mind.

Understand What to Practice and Which Success Conditioning Exercises Vastly Improve Performance

Just like your body needs to work out physically to stay in top shape, your brain needs a workout also. By practicing mental conditioning exercises, your brain will develop self-affirming thoughts and a higher-level of self-confidence almost automatically. Soon, positive thoughts and mental images will become a habit, and your brain will automatically be programmed for success.

As you previously learned, our thoughts can affect our lives in many ways. What we think we eventually do or become, and positive thoughts will only allow for positive experiences and outcomes. Our thoughts affect our emotions, which affect our actions, which affect our goals. Harboring negative thoughts leads to negative emotions, which lead to negative actions, or sometimes inaction. On the opposite end of the spectrum, positive thoughts lead to positive emotions, which lead to positive actions, which leads us to achieve our goals and increase our self-confidence.

Practicing good mental conditioning not only keeps us mentally and physically healthy, but also improves our self-confidence, increases our ability to concentrate, and reduces stress. Mental conditioning takes practice, but if you believe it, you can achieve it. By now you have learned that the mind is a powerful tool that you have with you at all times. When you are in peak mental condition, your self-confidence improves because you know you can achieve your goals. You can concentrate because you have a goal in mind and you know what it takes to achieve that goal. Your stress levels are down because you have an end goal in mind and have taken the steps to perform the end goal. You know what needs to be done and you have pictured yourself achieving said goal. Your feelings of stress and anxiety have all but disappeared because you are no longer frantic about achieving success and living your dreams. You know exactly what you need to accomplish to get there. This might sound like a foreign language to you, or at the very least, a little far-fetched. If you have just recently decided your brain and mental state could use a workout, then the following tips will be very beneficial to you. If you have been coaching yourself along the way, keep reading, as a refresher course is always a good reminder of how you can improve your thoughts and increase your mental strength so that you can achieve even more than you thought possible.

Take away surrounding factors so that you are forced into a new experience. This might sound unpleasant to you at first, but by removing external factors and pushing yourself to try something new, you have already taken a step forward out of your comfort zone. You will surprise yourself with what you can accomplish. For example, let's say you just started going to the gym. You might have been an athlete back in high school, but the obligations of a house, career, and family have gotten in the way of your fitness routine, and now you must backtrack to regain progress. Congratulations! The first step is knowing that you need to make a change. You have been working out at the gym in small increments of time, running on the treadmill and using the elliptical machine. Your friend is running a 5K and suggests that you should run with her next month. You are unsure how you feel about running in front of people and do not feel like you can compete, but against your better judgment, you sign up. You have already taken that first step out of your comfort zone. The first step is often the hardest, so there is nowhere to go but up from here. You begin to train so that you can run the entire three-point-one miles without stopping. You imagine yourself crossing the finish line and receiving the medal passed out by the race organization. Race day arrives, and you pace yourself appropriately and take it one mile at a time. You do successfully cross the finish line with a much faster time than you thought possible. Congratulations, again! You have forced yourself out of your comfort zone, tried a new experience, and felt a sense of accomplishment when you crossed the finish line. By breaking the race into manageable segments and picturing yourself succeeding, you did exactly that. You will surprise yourself with what you can accomplish when you put your mind to it and picture success.

Stick to a routine. Mental toughness and routine go hand in hand. Sticking to a routine is an important part of maintaining mental toughness. By sticking to a routine, you can plan out your day and allow for time if something does not go as planned. Creating your own routine allows you take control of your day and your schedule so that you can make the necessary changes. Keeping your routine and then crossing things off your list as you go through your day gives you a feeling of accomplishment and also boosts your self-confidence. Your feeling of success and accomplishment is directly related to your mental strength.

Don't let things bother you that you have no control over. We all have busy lives, and sometimes you just have to roll with the punches. We don't know what is going on in anyone else's head at any given point in time. That person who cut you off in traffic? They could very well have been late to pick up a sick kid from school. The person glaring at you at the grocery store? They might have been annoyed that the store was out of their favorite brand of salad dressing and just happened to be glaring in your direction as you walked by. The point is, we can only control our own actions and emotions, and if we let the actions and emotions of other people dictate our lives, we would never accomplish anything. Mentally strong people know that they control their own destiny and that it's up to themselves to take action and control of the situation. Situations in our workplace, the weather, and how others treat us are results of external factors, but mentally strong people know it's how we react to those situations that help improve our mental strength.

Get Rid of Limiting Beliefs and the Negative Critic in Your Head Once and For All

It is often said that we are our own worst critics. While we are sure that people are looking at us and criticizing or making fun, the reality of it is that no one is probably paying that much attention to what you see as imperfections. A mentally strong person will get rid of their self-limiting beliefs and not dwell on negative things. Eliminate those negative thoughts by replacing the thoughts with positive images and self-affirming language. Negative thoughts come from the feeling that you are losing control of a situation and will flounder in the aftermath. Negative thoughts also come from a feeling of uncertainty and the fear of the unknown. When something unexpected happens, such as a job loss, we do not know what will happen next. The unknown is scary, and the feeling of uncertainty is what causes the anxious feeling. A mentally strong person will take action to view yet another change as a challenge, and will take steps to derail their negative train of thought.

Alter your body language. Altering body language is a quick fix to eliminate that pesky internal critic. Stand up straight, uncross your arms, and hold your head tall. A confident posture will trick your mind and body into believing that you are confident.

Make a list of things to be thankful for. While it may be easy to get caught up in negative images, there is plenty around you to be thankful for. Make a list of things that you have accomplished recently or a list of people and things in your life for which you are grateful. Writing things down gives your brain a chance to brainstorm and think creatively, which will improve your self-image and bring about positive thoughts.

Do something creative. Start a craft project or work in your garden. Using your creativity boosts self-confidence and improves your mood. Once your creative juices are flowing, and you are completing an activity that you enjoy, your brain will recognize this and produce the appropriate chemicals to make you feel happy. When you are doing something creative, your self-confidence increases and your happiness returns. Happiness attracts happiness, and your negative thoughts and self-doubt will soon disappear.

A final way to get rid of these negative thoughts is to replace these thoughts with positive, self-affirming thoughts. Allow yourself to feel the negative thought and recognize why you feel that way or are feeling this sense of fear, and then replace the thought with a positive one. Picture yourself grabbing the thought and releasing it, then replace the thought with a positive thought that gives you a more desirable outcome. If you

are afraid, you will trip in front of a crowd of
people, release that thought from your head and
picture yourself walking calmly in front of the
crowd and straight to your destination.

Eliminating negative thoughts and training your
brain to think positively is something that comes
over time. You must first recognize when you are
thinking negative thoughts and determine what
is causing the thoughts to enter your head. By
practicing these techniques, they will soon
become a habit. Mentally strong people know
that it is up to them to embrace these challenges
and change their lives for the better.

Chapter 4:
Improve Focus and Concentration for Positive Results with Battle Training Mental Techniques

It is a well-known fact that members of any branch of the military today are some of the most battle-hardened, top-conditioned people in the country. Military personnel go through a grueling training program that produces some of the most mentally and physically tough people in our country. To complete these programs, the prospective soldier must first be emotionally intelligent and have strong mental health. He or she will use these qualities to complete their training and become even stronger, both physically and mentally, than they were before. Just as soldiers are trained in this manner, top professional athletes are trained in this manner as well. A professional athlete lives, breathes, dreams his or her sport, and just endures grueling days of physical challenges to revel in the spotlight of a two-hour game.

Gain Insight into the Coaching Psychology Behind Redirecting Anger Energy

Anger shows itself on many different levels. Some people are more apt to show anger than others. Although anger can be viewed as a negative emotion with a negative connotation, in truth, anger can be used for good when it is directed the right way. Everyone feels anger, but it is what we do with that anger that can determine the outcome.

When anger is used in a negative manner, it can halt success because too much time is wasted on feeling the emotion. People who cannot control their anger often pause what they are doing, feel the rage, and then are forced to redirect their attention back to the task at hand. When anger is used positively, the surge of energy and adrenaline that is felt in the heat of the moment can be used for good.

A bad call by a ref, an un-sportsmanlike play from an opposing teammate, or even personal error can cause many athletes to feel extreme anger, especially if surrounding circumstances dictate a stressful situation. A big game or tournament or a tough competitor can be just the thing that causes everyone's adrenaline to run high from the beginning. When extenuating circumstances are added to the mix, the first emotion many athletes feel, especially if they are competitive by nature, is anger. When playing sports, coaches often teach athletes to use their anger for good, using the energy as an extra boost to run the extra ten yards, pick up the pace down the court, or spike the volleyball that much harder.

Create an image in your head that will get you through anything. This image is often referred to as the "trigger." The trigger can be anything from your child, to your pet, to your best friend. This trigger is something that you live for and would do anything for. You can redirect your anger by thinking of this trigger to propel you through a difficult situation. Many military personnel envisions this image in their mind to get through a difficult situation or training. The thought of the person or animal at the end of the obstacle often propels the person through and gives them the extra surge of energy needed to complete the difficult task or the strength to go on in difficult times. Coaches instill this same idea by advising their athletes to pick a "trigger" as well. Not only does this technique get athletes through a grueling workout, but it allows the athletes to envision success. Coaches instruct their athletes to picture this trigger in the stands or watching the difficult workout take place. This, in turn, motivates most people to improve their performance, based on the sheer fact that their brain believes this. The athlete will perform better "knowing" that someone whom they are trying to impress is watching them.

Become aware of the situation. Military commanders and coaches alike instill this into their subjects. A tried and true battle technique is to become aware of your surroundings at all times, even if this just means glancing around and observing people in the surrounding area. By becoming aware of the surrounding situation, you can be ready for anything that might happen. All branches of the military instill this in their soldiers because it is important to be alert at all times if a dangerous situation would occur. Coaches instill this in their players as a part of the game. If athletes are aware of other players around them, they can anticipate not only the opponent's next move but their own next move as well. An emotionally intelligent person can observe and identify a situation, determine what they are feeling and why they are feeling these emotions, due to the situation, and then process their emotions and react accordingly. Becoming aware of your surrounding situations is something that comes with a practiced sense of self-awareness. You can practice this technique in any public place, regardless of whether or not you are in a situation that will make you angry. Next time you are sitting in a restaurant, take some time to observe others around you. Do those people sitting near you seem nervous, jittery, or full of energy? Are they tired and sluggish? Are you sitting in close proximity to someone, and if so, does that make you nervous? As you observe and analyze people around you, take note of your own reactions to your situation. Note your feelings and try to determine why you might be feeling what you are feeling. The more in tune you become with yourself, the easier it is to determine why you feel what you are feeling, and how you can use those emotions and reactions to your benefit. The mentally strong person can recognize his or her emotions and can also determine what is making them feel that way.

Use Anger Energy to Strengthen and Resolve Control

Anger is one of the most intense emotions that humans experience, and this can be both good and bad. That extra surge of energy you feel when you are angry can be used to accomplish new things or push yourself farther, as long as you use the feeling in the right way. Of course, too much anger is not a good thing. You know yourself better than anyone, and you can use your self-awareness to determine whether or not your anger is at a normal level for yourself. If you are someone who has an extreme temper and you know you get angry easily, check yourself from time to time to see if this is a normal feeling for you. If the feeling is not normal, check your circumstances and determine what changes can be made before your anger gets out of hand.

Don't become calm. Although this advice may sound counterintuitive, if you truly want to use your anger to produce a positive outcome, trying to calm yourself down completely will not produce the desired effect. The rage you feel is what will cause you to make a change in your life or complete an action. For example, as an athlete, if you had possession of the ball and had been tackled the last three times you ran down the field, you can use this anger to fuel your energy to run faster. A mentally strong person will not get discouraged by this setback of being tackled; rather, he will use this chance to improve his playing skills and will be motivated to run faster. He will picture himself in the end zone, dancing his victory dance after he scores a touchdown. He will imagine how it would feel to hear the crowd cheering, he will imagine how the turf smells, and he will imagine the scoreboard changing, his team's score increasing after he has made the touchdown. He might even go so far as to imagine how the ice-cold water will taste after he runs fast enough to score the touchdown. The moral of the story is, by trying to calm your emotions and remove some of the anger, you are losing some of the ammunition that will ultimately fuel your fire to accomplish your goal.

Use the anger to make a plan. Human beings are emotional creatures, and the anger you feel can be your drive and determination to make a plan.

If you are someone who gets annoyed easily, but never does anything to correct the situation, you can use your anger to make a plan. Do not try to calm yourself down, because once you are calm, you will most likely decide that the thing that once made you so angry is no longer a big deal. While your emotions are still running high and you still feel angry, make a plan that will get you out of the situation. If you are at work and your boss has incorrectly blamed you for a mistake, it is wise not to yell or direct the anger towards your boss. Rather, make a plan and use your anger to fuel your actions. Rewrite your cover letter, stating exactly what your qualifications are. Give up your hour of television time each night to begin searching for a new job. The bottom line is, if you try to calm yourself in every situation, you will not be able to reign in your anger to use it productively. Allow yourself to feel the anger, and remember the feelings you felt when the experience happened. Make the determination that you will not allow yourself to be put into this situation again, and resolve to change it. A mentally strong person knows some things in life cannot be controlled, but he or she can determine how they respond to the situation. Recognizing that the emotion they are feeling is anger, identifying the source of the anger, and then making the determination to resolve the solution are all signs of behavior that an emotionally intelligent human being would display.

Decide if it's worth showing your anger. Some things in life are just not worth getting upset about. While it's great to use your anger to make necessary changes in your life, sometimes it is just as important to step back and decide whether or not it is worth getting upset about the situation at hand. An emotionally intelligent person can look at the situation and determine why they are feeling the way they are, and then decide if their emotions are warranted. A good way to put this practice into perspective is to ask yourself how you would feel if someone close to you was telling you the same story. If a close friend or family member had the same scenario happen to them, and they recounted the story to you, how would you feel? Would you be enraged on their behalf, or would you think they were overreacting? This can sometimes be an effective tool in determining whether it is a good idea to use your anger to make a change, or if you should just let the situation drop. An emotionally intelligent person can make the determination between rational and irrational behavior.

Use Proven Sports Technology Techniques to Leave Your Ego Outside

When most people hear the word ego, there is a negative connotation that comes to mind. You might think of a famous musician or athlete who is portrayed in the media as very full of themselves. You might also hear the word ego and think of someone who has an inflated ego, or a big ego. Truthfully, everyone has an ego, but it's when the ego becomes too inflated that problems arise. The ego is your own sense of self-esteem and importance. Some people tend to have high egos and extremely high levels of self-esteem, while still, other people tend to have lower egos and low levels of self-esteem. While it is good to have a sense of self-worth, an overly inflated ego can be annoying to others around you, causing you to lose friends and make family members dread being around you. No one wants to hear about how great you are or how wonderful your athletic ability is every time they see you, but at the same time, an emotionally intelligent and mentally strong person has a great sense of self and a high level of self-esteem. How can we determine the difference, and when our ego gets in the way, how can we leave our ego outside and enter the ring of life in a more humble state?

One way to determine whether someone has an over-active ego is to decide whether or not that person can back up what they are saying with their actions. If a star athlete brags about their skills, yet doesn't deliver peak performance when he is on the basketball court, then his over-inflated ego is getting in the way of this performance and is also hurting his teammates. If the star athlete not only brags about his skills, but then does not deliver on the basketball court, is rude to his teammates and opponents, and disrespectful to his coaches and superiors, then his ego has become over-inflated. As a general rule of thumb, if someone can practice good sportsmanship, they have a high level of confidence and a healthy ego. And in real life, typically someone who is friendly, can get along with others, and can place themselves in others' shoes is someone who has a high confidence level and a healthy ego. Emotionally intelligent and mentally strong people can maintain their self-confidence, yet still participate in competitive activities. They can recognize their emotions and realize when they are feeling a negative emotion, and what might be causing them to feel this way.

While high levels of self-confidence are good, an over-inflated ego is not. There are some proven ways to drop the ego and return to your more humble bearings, and like most strategies used to improve your mental state, these too require practice and patience.

Practice forgiveness. Recognize that not everyone is out to get you. Everyone that you encounter on a daily basis is human, just like you. Circumstances will occur throughout your day that might offend you, but it is how you react to these circumstances that dictate the level of your mental state. Whether someone has intended to offend you or not, practice forgiveness. Forgiving someone for a wrongdoing, whether real or imagined, has a calming effect. It is natural to be upset if someone slams the door in your face or pulls out in front of you at the intersection, but not recognizing that this could be an honest mistake is detrimental to your physical and mental health. If you feel the need to chase the co-worker down the hall at work to in turn slam the door in his face, or chase the offending driver down the street to honk and wave at them, it is time to check your ego. Letting these small things drop and moving on with your day are proveen ways to set your ego aside. You do not always have to be right, and you do not always have to come out on top of every situation.

Additionally, your ego can benefit from forgiving bigger transgressions as well. If a friend or family member unintentionally offended you and then apologizes, you can practice keeping your ego in check by choosing to forgive them. Everyone makes mistakes, and the emotionally healthy and mentally strong person can recognize this and move on with their lives. At the same time, the emotionally healthy person is also able to set boundaries and stand up for themselves, so if this person keeps offending you, you owe it to yourself to enforce the consequences and move on with your life. Forgive the person and realize that you deserve to be treated with respect. It is when you throw a temper tantrum and try to get even with the offending person that the negative side of your ego comes out, causing others to feel like you have an over-inflated sense of self.

One way to keep your ego at a healthy level is to realize you can't control every situation. Every situation in life will not go as planned. The emotionally intelligent person realizes this and makes amends to their plan when they need to, viewing obstacles as new challenges and not complete disasters. People who only want to do things their way, remaining rigid and unchanging, are not allowing themselves to grow as a person. Someone with an over-inflated ego only wants things to be done their way, regardless of how many other people are involved in the decision-making process. By stepping back, letting some things happen naturally, and embracing the challenges that life throws at you, your ego will stay outside, allowing you to enter and experience all life has to offer.

Conclusion

Improving Mental Toughness Will Benefit Every Area of Your Life

Mental toughness is a key component to living a successful, healthy life. It is normal for everyone to experience setbacks in life, and sometimes we go through a period of time in our lives that is more challenging than other times. It is what we do with these challenges that can vastly impact our lives. By achieving and maintaining a high level of emotional intelligence, we can recognize and alter our reactions to fit the situation, as well as to benefit ourselves in the long run. By practicing the acts of believing and relying on our intuition, setting boundaries, adhering to a schedule, and eliminating the fear of rejection, we can effectively reduce anxiety and in turn, boost self-esteem.

When things do not go our way, we can choose to use these unfavorable opportunities as a chance to grow and change, or we can choose to let ourselves be struck down by these situations, remaining in a rut and feeling stuck. When we have too many negative circumstances in our lives, it is only natural for us to feel the intense emotion of anger, but it is what we do with that anger that can turn our lives around for the better. Learning to harness our anger and use this extra energy can be a monumental, life-altering strategy. The practice of training your brain and using proven psychological techniques has been shown to be beneficial to athletes and military personnel, and you too can learn to employ these methods to improve the quality of your life, your self-esteem, and your overall mental health.

Improving your mental toughness will get you through a tough work day, will help you determine the appropriate response to adverse events, and will improve your overall self-confidence. Maintaining a high level of self-confidence is paramount to living a healthy, happy life. Improving your mental strength not only improves your life but the lives of others around you. Your friends and family will notice the change in your overall demeanor and your happiness, as will you. Happy people tend to attract happy people, and people who display a healthy ego, a high level of self-confidence, and terrific mental toughness are often more sought-after in the workplace. These same people also tend to make and keep true friendships and relationships, as they can set boundaries and enjoy a balance of personal time and time spent with others.

Mental toughness is not something that can be learned overnight; it takes practice and determination to change your mindset and adjust your way of thinking. The good news is, if you have found the need for improvement in your mental health, you have already taken a step in the right direction.

Cognitive Behavioral Therapy

————— ❧❧❧❧ —————

How to Combat Depression, Fear, Anxiety and Worry (Happiness can be trained)

Chris S Jennings

Table of Contents

Introduction

There are plenty of books on this subject on the market, thanks again for choosing this one! Every effort was made to ensure it is full of as much useful information as possible, please enjoy!

Depression and anxiety disorders depict a life driven by anxiety. It is an important part of being human. Every human being uses anxiety as a survival mechanism. It consists of a sequence of responses and reflexes which prepare us to stay out of danger. This is one of the reasons why we experience anxiety.

Most of the time it sits in the background until that point when we need it. However, for many people anxiety develops and becomes stronger for no good reason. It begins to show up frequently and in an intense manner. It can become more dominant and over time, it may result in serious problems such as unnecessary worry, panic attacks, feelings of apprehension, obsessive thoughts and compulsive behaviors.

Cognitive Behavioral Therapy

Continuous experience of anxiety, phobias, depression, and panic may leave us feeling hopeless and helpless. And there is nothing that can be done to free us from it. Years of reading books and websites, searching for what could be the answers, attempting to find ways to think, ways to behave, therapy, medication and many more can leave us feeling exhausted without a single hope and even very anxious.

And yet, many people successfully overcome all these troubles. Often after years and years of experience, experimenting and researching their problem. They discover the answer. They don't wake up one morning and find their problem is gone, no. Instead, they grow, let it go and change. Their problem vanishes when they begin to understand, build a different perspective and begin to behave differently. Each chapter of this book will help you learn different ways which you can overcome your fear, anxiety, and depression. The chapters have different step by step processes which you can follow to ensure that you combat your feelings of anxiety.

Chapter 1:
Understanding Depression, Fear, and Anxiety

Everyone has experienced depression at one point in their life. Each person's experience is different because the symptoms are not the same. Many people feel sad occasionally, or go through rough times, but they have certain areas in their life when they feel good and love specific aspects of themselves. However, this is not the same for some, life is more of a struggle. They feel sad about themselves and their lives. At times they feel completely hopeless. If you have ever felt this way, chances are that you might be depressed.

What is depression?

Most people often say "they feel depressed" to mean they are feeling sad or miserable about life. Usually, these feelings disappear after sometime. However, if the feelings are disrupting your life activity and continue to disturb you even after 2-

3 weeks, or they recur over and over again, for a few days at a time, you could be depressed.

Depression is a lengthy and persistent mood which can affect many aspects of one's life. It is characterized by feelings of sadness, loneliness, excessive guilt, and worthlessness. Other times you may even develop suicidal thoughts. A normal depression can extend for a few minutes to a few days. We have all gone through these periods of being "sad" or "down". These feelings are part of being human. But, when depression becomes extreme and goes beyond the normal periods of time, it is far from the everyday sort. For this extreme type of depression, you will need to consider getting help. There are different forms of depression:

- **Seasonal affective disorder (SAD)-** Just as the name suggests, this is a seasonal form of depression. It often appears in the winter and autumn, the time when days are short and the sun is low in the sky, and it starts to improve when the days get longer and brighter.

Chapter 1: Understanding Depression, Fear , and Anxiety

- **Postnatal depression-**many mothers experience the 'baby blues' immediately after giving birth to their baby, but it then disappears after 1-2 days. Postnatal depression is a more severe problem and can take place at any time either two weeks or two years after giving birth.

- **Bipolar disorder (Manic depression)-**Some people develop major mood swings when the periods of depression switch with the periods of mania. Mania is when they are in a high state of excitement and may attempt to do over-ambitious ideas and schemes. During this time, they have periods of severe depression.

- **Psychotic depression-** takes place when an individual has extreme types of depression.

- **Persistent depressive Disorder-**This is a form of depression which may extend for two years.

- **Major depression-** It is a form of depression characterized by severe symptoms that disrupt a person from working, sleeping, eating and enjoying life. An instance of major depression may occur once in a lifetime.

Symptoms and Signs that show up if you have depression

Sadness. There are certain people with depression who might not feel sad at all. Depression has many different types of symptoms, not forgetting to mention the physical symptoms. If you discover that you have any of the symptoms following lasting for more than 2 weeks, chances are that you have depression:

- Feeling of pessimism, hopelessness.

- Loss of interest participating in activities and hobbies.

- Persistent sadness, empty mood or anxiousness.

- Difficulty in making decisions, concentrating or remembering things.

- Feeling guilt, helplessness, and worthlessness.

- Continuous physical symptoms.

- A feeling of committing suicide

- Experiencing sleepless nights, oversleeping or insomnia.

- Loss of appetite and changes in weight.

- Restlessness and irritability.

- Turning to alcohol or drugs.

- Getting angry easily.

- Crying for no good reason.

Factors that contribute to Depression

Many different factors contribute to depression. It does not have a single cause. It can either be triggered or occur spontaneously without any relation to a physical illness, life crisis or other risks. Scientists have come up with various factors which they think may lead to depression:

- **Trauma.** When a person experiences trauma at an early stage, it can result in long-term changes in the way their brains respond to feelings of stress and fear. These changes in the brain can explain why people with a history of childhood trauma have a high probability of depression.

- **Genetics.** Suicide risks and mood disorders seem to run in families, however, genetic inheritance is only a single factor.

- **Life circumstances.** Financial status, marital status and the place a person is living play a certain role in determining whether a person may develop depression or not.

- **Structure of the brain.** Results from imaging studies indicate the frontal lobe of the brain becomes less active when a person feels depressed. Depression is further associated with changes in the way the pituitary gland and hypothalamus can respond to hormone stimulation.

- **Substance abuse.** Close to 30% of people who abuse drugs have depression.

- **Other medical conditions.** People who have a history of chronic pain, sleep disturbances, anxiety, attention-deficit hyperactivity disorder and medical illness are likely to have depression.

Depression doesn't care whether you are a child or a grown up, it can attack anyone at any age. However, in young children, it starts while they are in their early 20s. For the adults, anxiety disorders arise in the form of abnormal levels of anxiety. It also shows up together with a complicated medical illness like diabetes and heart diseases. Depression can worsen these conditions. In some cases, medication recommended for these illnesses may lead to side effects which cause depression.

How depression affects people

Depression affects people in many different ways. Certain symptoms might show up in a person and fail to appear in another person. Some people only experience a few symptoms of depression. Others have many symptoms. The scale of severity, the number of times the symptoms appear, and the period the symptoms are going to stay will change depending on the individual and the type of illness.

Women

Women with depression don't experience the same symptoms. However, depressed women have symptoms of guilt, sadness, and worthlessness.

Depression is prevalent amongst more women than men. Hormonal, biological, lifecycle and psychological factors are unique to women. This might be associated with their higher rate of depression. For example, most women are weak after giving birth, therefore, they are likely to suffer from postpartum depression.

Men

How men suffer from depression is very different from the ladies. Women who have depression may feel sad and worthless, men are not the same. For men, they lose interest and feel irritable. Some even have sleepless nights. Men might resort to drugs or alcohol when they feel depressed. They could also feel discouraged, frustrated, irritable, abusive and angry. There are certain men who get busy in their jobs as a mechanism to avoid speaking with their family friends about the problems which they are going through.

Children

Before they reach puberty, boys and girls have an equal chance to develop depression. Children who are feeling depressed might pretend to their parents that they are sick. Some stick to their parents while others decide not to go to school. Like men and women, the behaviors of children are also different. This means that it can be very difficult to tell if a child is suffering from depression. Other times the parent can be worried about the behavior of the child, or a teacher can notice that a child has changed in the way he or she normally behaves.

Teens

If there are difficult times for a person while growing up is when you are a teen. This is the time when you begin to develop your identity. There are a lot of issues which you seem to be at war with as a teen. Some of the main issues include sexuality and the ability to make independent decisions without external interference. Bad moods are predicted to affect a teen; however, depression might be different.

Children who are older and teens suffering from depression might sulk, be negative, irritable and find themselves in trouble at school. If you are not sure whether your teen is suffering from depression, you should measure the length of time the symptoms have persisted. Again, study the way your teen is behaving far from her normal self. They might also have a high likelihood of committing suicide.

Children and teenagers often depend on their parents, teachers, or any person that is older and mature enough to notice their suffering and help them recover from it. Many teens don't know what to do or where to seek help for mental treatment. Some have a perception that treatment won't help. Others don't seek help because they believe that the symptoms of depression are just part and parcel of the usual stress of being a teen at school. In some cases, teens feel terrified about the way the rest of the world is going to look at them when they look for further mental treatment.

Grownup People

Feeling depressed beyond the normal period is not a sign of oldness. In fact, many studies show that the older you get the more comfortable you feel. It is not easy to identify depression in aged people because they may not have clear symptoms.

Some older people with depression appear tired, have sleepless nights, or look grumpy and irritable. Attention problems as a result of depression might appear. Older adults could also experience medical conditions such as cancer, heart disease, and stroke, which might trigger depressive symptoms. Or they might be taking medications which have side effects that lead to depression.

Some older adults could experience what doctors refer to as vascular depression. This occurs when the blood vessels in the body harden and stiffen. Now, when the blood vessels get stiff, they acts as a barrier in allowing the normal flow of blood to the rest of the other body organs. Those people who suffer from vascular depression have a high risk for stroke or heart disease.

Sometimes it becomes difficult to differentiate grief from major depression. Experiencing sorrow when your close family member passes on is a common symptom that does not need professional help. However, extended grief is not normal. It could mean the person is severely depressed. Adults growing old have a higher chance to suffer from depression especially if they once went through it while they were young.

Understanding Fear and anxiety

Fear and anxiety are something most people experience in the course of life. However, having just some anxiety is good because it can help people to get ready for challenges, difficult situations, and deal with dangers.

Fear is a powerful emotion. It has a very strong influence on your body and mind. Fear can trigger strong signals of response when we're in emergencies. For instance, if we are being attacked. Fear can also invade us when we are asked to stand and deliver a speech to a big crowd of people or about to sit for exams.

Chapter 1: Understanding Depression, Fear , and Anxiety

Anxiety is a term we use to refer to some types of fear having to do with the thought of a danger or something going wrong in the future. Fear and anxiety can occur for a short time and then disappear, but they can also extend for a longer time and you can get disturbed with them. Sometimes, fear and anxiety can take over your life, interfere with your eating cycle, travel, sleep, concentration, or even going to school or work. This can stop you from doing things that you want to do, appreciate doing, and also affect your health.

Some people are taken over by fear and want to avoid situations that may make them anxious. It can be difficult to put an end to this cycle, but there are lots of ways to do it.

However, certain forms of anxiety are common in a person's life:

- **Infants aged 18-months** have a stranger anxiety. It is a normal and common type of anxiety which many young children have when they are standing or sitting close to strangers. This makes the young children want to stay near their parents. Furthermore, this is healthy and protective for an infant to have since it helps them stay close to their parents.

- **Kids between 2-6** are petrified of monsters, darkness, and giants.

- **Kids age 7-12** are fearful of losing their parent or even bad things that could happen to them.

- **Teenagers experience** social fears of getting accepted and fitting in the complicated social life of a teenager.

When a person has so much anxiety to the point where it interferes with their normal life and prevents them from doing certain things, then it is referred to as an Anxiety Disorder or Anxiety Condition.

Symptoms of anxiety

Some of the common symptoms that people may experience when they are anxious include:

Physical sensations

- Poor concentration
- Dry mouth
- Feeling dizzy
- Diarrhea
- Low energy
- Frequent urination
- Rapid heartbeat
- Difficulty swallowing
- Pain in chest
- Discomfort in the abdomen

Emotional or Psychological symptoms

- Irritability
- Insomnia
- Feeling unreal
- Fear that you are losing it
- Difficulty concentrating

Major types of Anxiety Conditions

There are different forms of anxiety situations that people can experience:

Generalized Anxiety Disorder. A kid suffering from this form of disorder will have a hard time managing their fears, this means that they will become petrified of everything. Excessive worries lead to stress on the body. So, this type of disorder also has physical symptoms such as fatigue, irritability, difficulty concentrating, restlessness, sleep problems and muscle tension.

Obsessive Compulsive Disorder. The condition may have repetitive and distressing:

- Obsessions-thoughts or images

- Compulsions-habits that one can't resist and feels pressured to do.

A classic example of obsessions includes obsession of cleanliness, which results in a compulsion of cleaning or handwashing repetitively.

Panic disorder. These are recurrent impulsive episodes of panic that are related to physiological and psychological symptoms. Physical symptoms include breathing problems, chest pain, and dizziness. Some of the psychological and behavior symptoms consist of extreme fear, and the need to run away from the condition causing panic.

Phobias. Most people experience phobias when they are scared of a specific thing such as snakes, storms etc.

Social phobia. This is fear of social situations where the person stands before unfamiliar people. It is beyond normal shyness. It prevents people from attaining their full potential at work and school because of their behaviors to avoid school, social or work situations.

Post-traumatic stress disorder. This is a delayed reaction to a traumatic situation such as a house on fire, car accident, or being hurt by others through bullying. The person might relive the situation, and have nightmares, flashbacks or deep emotions. The person might be on edge all the time, with sleep problems and low concentration and energy.

Selective Mutism. This is the failure to speak in certain social situations such as school while speaking in other social places such as at home.

Separation anxiety disorder. It is an excessive anxiety about separation from a parent or caregiver that is not right according to the child's developmental level and age. For instance, a 2-year old getting nervous about being detached from their parent is usual, but a 7-year old with the same signs would be abnormal.

Common Anxiety Situations for Children

Some of the common triggering events for children include:

- Farewell from a loved one

- Social fears like interacting with new friends, scoring good grades and encountering with new people.

- Performance anxiety such as public speaking, speaking in front of the class, writing exams or tests.

- Academic stress from the need to get good grades.

- Worries about the things that may happen such as "What if ...."

- Teasing or bullying by others.

What do fear and anxiety feel like?

When you are frightened or extremely anxious, your mind and body operate quickly. These are some of the things that may happen:

- Fast heartbeat

- Having dry mouth

- You have a loose bowel

- You sweat a lot

- You can't concentrate on one particular thing

- You remain frozen in one place

The above things could occur because whenever your body develops a sense of fear, it begins to prepare yourself for an emergency. It is this getting ready for the emergency that results in increased blood flow around your body muscles and increased level of concentration on the thing that seems to be a threat.

With the feeling of anxiety, you may experience some of the above symptoms as well as a nagging sense of fear, and you may become irritable, experience sleep problems, develop headaches, or experience problems going to work and planning for the future.

Steps of Anxiety

The cognitive-behavioral model for anxiety has different stages:

1. Triggering event
2. Thoughts
3. Feelings
4. Behaviors

Chapter 1: Understanding Depression, Fear , and Anxiety

1. **Triggering Event.** Anxiety begins after a triggering event. For instance, a child with anxiety is waiting to see her parent after school, but the parent is delayed.

2. **Thoughts.** The next stage is the person with anxiety experiences anxiety thoughts or thoughts of worry. Often, the thoughts revolve around two major themes:

   a. A feeling of powerlessness, or

   b. The world is a threatening place

3. **Feelings.** Thoughts of anxiety result in anxiety feelings, which vary in the level of severity. We have mild worry, anxiety, then sheer panic.

4. **Behaviors**. A common practice when one is feeling anxious is to run away from the danger that makes people avoid their fears. However, running away from fear doesn't help, but only adds salt to the problem in the future.

Chapter 2:
Setting goals and lifestyle changes

M any of us have been in a state where we've set goals but then failed to accomplish them. The passion may have been present and we had the best intentions, but nothing happened. Life got busy and we forgot all about our goals. Then, as time passed by, we were reminded of our goals, we discovered that we are not closer to achieving our goals.

Goal setting in therapy, and its importance

When it comes to setting goals in therapy, one must identify some of the outcomes they want to achieve. It is important that the goals are measurable, achievable as well as observable. Furthermore, the goals must relate to the behavioral changes or cognitive changes of the present problem. Goals extend the period of sessions, allow one to perform the specific treatment. This gives time for the therapist to measure the improvements.

Cognitive behavioral therapy(CBT) consists of a goal-oriented treatment method in itself. Focused on changing the behavior, patterns of thinking, as well as the attitude one might have towards the challenges they are facing.

When it comes to setting goals, a CBT therapist might help you:

- Identify the goal
- Concentrate on the performance and not just the outcome
- Discover the difference and connection between short-term and long-term goals.
- Have goals which are said to be S.M.A.R.T goals.

Identify the goal

It is important to have your goal identified. Let's say that you have the set goal to complete a marathon. If you set a clear vision about this goal, you will:

- Understand what the goal is and why it is important to achieve it.

- What are some of the hardships that can take place?

If you work with a CBT therapist, he or she can help you concentrate on your strengths and let you gain positive attitude right from the start.

Long-term or short-term goal?

Something else that a CBT will help you is to understand the link and difference between long-term and short-term goals. If you want to participate in a marathon, it is not enough to buy running shoes and then wait for the day of the marathon to arrive. No!

When you put your focus on achieving your goals, chances are that you will achieve the outcome goal. This doesn't mean now you should forget about the main goal. The secret is to learn how to maintain your focus, and balance between the two.

Assessing Barriers, Facilitators, Importance and Confidence

Once multiple goals or a single goal has been achieved, it is important for the therapist to examine the situation of the patient and attitude about the goals. For instance, a therapist should ask for some little details of the patient's life which may act in preventing them from achieving their goal. A resilient family together with a mature social-support structure might help a patient to accomplish their goals.

An assessment of importance and confidence are also critical. A therapist should make a request to the patient to let her rate the level of importance of their or her own goal. The scale should run from 0-100. A scale of 0 should mean that the goal is not that important while a rate of 100 means the goal is very important.

The therapist should then discuss with the patient if the ratings are below 60. The patient together with the therapist must sit down and re-evaluate the goals. The therapist could ask the patient to tell him or her the level of confidence. It is good if you can give freedom to the patient to say their or her confidence in choosing the goal.

Tips to use when setting the goals

- **Explain the basis for why you need to set the goals.** By following this route, you will help the patient to develop an understanding of the treatment. Plus, it shapes the patient to have a clear view of how much commitment she needs.

- **Highlight desired results.** This consists of the therapist helping you define your goals and specify reasons for coming for the treatment.

- **Be Specific about your goal.** Perform a deep analysis of each goal. This involves discovering the objective of each goal. Guide the patient so that they may find the right path in discovering goals that they may require to modify.

- **List goals by adopting a positive trend.** This will help the patient to outline goals which they prefer to accomplish rather than what they don't want to.

- **Measure the merits and drawbacks of a goal.** This will help understand some of the negatives and positives of accomplishing this goal. In any cases, it helps in understanding the financial budget that might be involved. Furthermore, it works as an inspiration to the patient who has not yet made a decision.

- **Write down some of the behaviors linked to the goal**. This action helps the patient to see the importance of getting involved in a given activity. To help the patient have a chance to succeed, it is important to define goals which are possible to achieve. Don't try to do only one thing daily. This makes everything hard to achieve.

- **Evaluate symptoms regularly**. Monitor the way the goals reduce mental h symptoms and improve the activeness and quality of life.

When thinking about goal setting, it is important to think about the things in life that you enjoy or value. The concept behind goal setting in CBT is that you are working towards something that will enhance your mood, assist you to connect with the things which are important to you and award you for the efforts you have put in. So, instead of thinking about goals that might be a result of self-critical thinking, start to think about things that are significant to you.

Once you have a hint about your goal and what you want to achieve, it is good to make sure that is specific. If you have a specific goal, it will guide you to know exactly what you need to do, and for how long you might need to spend doing it. This way, you can tell when you have accomplished your goal.

Your therapist can help you set goals and work towards making it a reality, but if you already developed an idea about the goals you wanted to work towards, this will help you to set the ball rolling.

Life Style Changes

Is your life packed with so many things to do and too little time? Are you the kind of person who takes dinner at the nearest restaurant before you go home? Do you experience sleepless nights? If you are living a life where you are eating a poor diet, doing limited exercise or one where you don't get enough sleep, perhaps it is why you are feeling depressed.

This section will take you through three quality strategies to calm your life. We shall further help you rediscover the enthusiasm for getting back to doing those morning exercises every day.

Designing Calming diets

Why you need to eat healthily

Everybody needs to make a choice to improve their diet. We consider a person to be eating a healthy meal if it has all the nutrients. Most people don't know that eating a balanced diet has many advantages. Some of the benefits that you get when you choose to eat a meal that contains all nutrients include reducing the chances of getting obesity

Many people across the world like foods that have a higher percentage of calories. This is not recommended at all. In fact, if your level of calories intake is higher than the rate at which your body is burning calories, you have a higher chance to add a lot of weight. So, you need to make sure that you consume calories depending on the level of activeness of your body.

Another important thing to consider when you aim to eat a balanced diet, make sure you don't just eat a meal which has three types of nutrients. Instead, eat a complete meal which will provide your body with all the nutrients that you deserve.

At times, if your moods are not ok you may get tempted to eat excessively. This often happens with the ladies. Some even decide to eat foods which contain high amounts of sugar and fat.

But, did you know that eating for the sake of your emotions doesn't last for a long time? Most of the time it only lasts for an hour or so. The long-term effect of having a poor diet is that you become much depressed.

Go for the little portion

Nowadays, the amount of food that people tend to eat has increased in size. Many people eat much compared to the people who lived before us. If you are among those people who can't just eat the right amount of food. You can use the following tips to improve yourself.

Cognitive Behavioral Therapy

- **Get a smaller plate.** Sometimes all it takes for you to eat the right size is to buy a small plate. Using a smaller plate makes your mind to think that you have eaten a lot.

- **Don't eat fast.** It is always recommended for one to eat slowly. This gives more time for your stomach and the brain to communicate when you need to stop eating.

- **Serve food once.** When it comes to eating, just serve yourself once and keep away the dishes with the remaining food. This trick prevents you from wanting to serve yourself food again.

- **Eating in a restaurant**. Remember that the meals in a restaurant are twice the normal meals we take daily. This means that you should not eat all the meal yourself. If you are seated in the restaurant with a friend, you can allocate him or her some of it.

Adopt a nutrition formula

There are people who opt to eat several types of food such as French fries and ketchup to enhance their low moods. One of the reasons for this is because these foods are rich in carbohydrates. Their body has a good mechanism to transform the carbohydrates into sugar and consume it. This fast rate of food conversion results in a rapid drop of blood sugar. The resulting effect includes an increase in sugar cravings.

So, instead of eating foods which have carbohydrates, one should go for foods rich in fiber and carbs so that they can boost the levels of blood sugar. Complex carbs exist in vegetables, whole grains, and legumes.

Never skip breakfast

Breakfast has been considered by many to be the most essential meal that every human being should ensure that they don't miss. By just eating breakfast, you can control your weight. Whole meal cereal is recommended since it is a nutritious diet to start your day.

Take five portions of fruit and vegetables

You should aim to consume a minimum of five fruits every day. Other diets like fruit juice without sugar and vegetables added to meals play a role. Include a fruit in each of your breakfasts if you want to make sure you are taking a healthy meal.

Eat a lot of fish

Try to eat two portions of fish every week. Fish is very rich in proteins, vitamins as well as minerals which contribute to your overall health. Only salmon, sardines, fresh tuna, and mackerel are rich in the omega-3 fats. Omega-3 fats are beneficial to the body, besides preventing complex problems related to the heart, they help cure other related diseases.

Include starch diet

Certain types of foods such as rice, cereals, potatoes and many others contribute to a large percentage of your diet. It is a good practice to have this diet into your meal. You should not forget to add whole grain to your diet also. Whole grain is foods which have a higher percentage of fiber.

Reduce the intake of sugar and fat

To stay healthy, make sure you eliminate saturated fats from your list. Foods rich in saturated fats are dangerous to your body. They are among the leading causes of heart disease. If you can purchase vegetable oil, go for it. Eat lean meat. Instead of buying foods which contain higher amounts of fat, buy avocados and oily fish which are free from unsaturated fats.

Reduce your levels of sugar consumption

If there is one thing which you need to pay much attention is taking drinks with a high concentration of sugar. These drinks are some of the factors which will make you add in weight. Instead of taking processed drinks, eat foods which have natural sugar.

Reduce the levels of salt consumption

Excessive consumption of salt is dangerous to your body; it might lead to blood pressure. Limit the amount of salt that you put in your food. Another way you can ensure that you don't take much salt is to avoid eating processed foods. Always make sure you read the food labels to note down the level of salt. Don't forget that food such as bacon and cheese contain a higher percentage of salt. However, many people don't take time to consider this fact.

Family and friends

Our family members can help us a lot to cope with our anxiety and fear. They can be there to do what they can to offer us guidance, listen to some of the issues we go through and many more. On the other hand, they can also make us want to run away and hide because of some of the demands they present to us.

Sometimes they complain about problems which they are the authors of the same problems, leaving you feeling depressed and tired. In this section, we will look at the merits and drawbacks of having people in your life and some of the ways in which you can benefit from their relationships. Remaining connected to others.

Remaining connected to others

As much as friends and our close relatives can stress us, many studies still support the role that a good family relationship does in improving the overall state of a person. To stay connected with your family friends relieves the mental state of an individual. Good relationship reduces mental stress.

Therefore, any time you seem to be worried or even depressed, getting in touch with your close friends can help you fight stress. Speaking with the people you love helps relieve pain and negative thoughts about life. Some of the tips you can apply include:

- Meeting physically with your friends is a sure way of staying connected.

- Eat together with your close family members. Make jokes and have fun.

- Volunteer to help your community or school

- Look for the phone numbers of those friends whom you haven't spoken for a while and call them.

- Walk around your neighborhood and make new friends. Get to know the people whom you share similar values.

- Volunteer to help your relatives who may be having problems. You can clean their compound if it is dirty.

From the above tips, to stay in touch with your friends does not need you to spend a lot of money. All you need to set a side is the time and effort. This effort will benefit both you and the people you visit.

However, most people who are going through social anxiety might experience a big problem when dealing with this issue. But, you only need to start small. Get in touch with one person, it could be your brother, cousin or even your long time classmate. If you are that person who believes you can't get time to interact with your family friends. The next section will help you discover ways in which you can set time.

Allocate designated time for interaction

Many people who suffer from anxiety are never secure when they delegate any task to someone else. They believe that without any of their efforts, the end result will fall short of their required standards. I guess this has ever happened to you one time. But, what should you do when you are depressed to the point where you cannot perform your duties. Whether you like it or not, you will need to learn how to assign some tasks for people to help you. If you struggle to deliver when you are under a lot of stress, chances are that you are going to mess up everything. Besides that, your level of anxiety is going to increase. So, assigning some tasks to your friends to help you always solve the problem.

Here are tips to read when you want to delegate your tasks:

- Trust your partner to help you in some of the duties at home

- Hire a rental service to come and help in cleaning your compound.

- Spend some time let's say on a Sunday to prepare a meal which you can eat the next week.

- Ensure that you enroll in online banking. This will help you save the time of travelling to the bank to pay your monthly bills.

- Speak to one of your family members so that he or she can participate in a communal cleaning service.

As you can see, it is very simple to delegate some of the tasks. You don't need to do it yourself. All you need to do is to be confident and hopeful that you the person you have requested to step in for you will do an excellent job. In addition, some of these ideas may require you to cash in some money. For instance, if you want to hire a rental cleaning company, you will need to pay the company some fees for the services. You may look at this as a costly idea, but in the long run, it is worthy because you will get time to rest.

When it comes to assigning tasks, it is also good if you can give some guidance to the person so that they do a wonderful job. Delegating some of your tasks will relieve you from the burdens of life that you are going through. This then helps reduce stress and depression.

Teach yourself to say no

Most people who are anxious don't know when to say no. Majority of the times they find themselves accepting to perform a given task whenever requested. Anxiety is never a good feeling; it prevents an individual from disclosing their real feelings. Whenever this happens, the end result is anger and frustration. Plus, if you don't learn to resist certain requests, there are people who will take advantage of your situation. This means you are going to get overworked.

So, if you would like to handle this situation, you need to first identify scenarios which you always accept requests when it is not from your own heart. It could be happening while you are at work, with your family friends or even when you are in a new environment. The next time people ask you to do them a favor or something which you are not comfortable. Follow these steps:

Think about the request. For example, if John is going to ask you to buy for him a bottle of soda while you are coming to work, you tell him like this, "I understand that it would be more convenient for you if I bought for you the bottle of soda". The trick with this move is that you will get time to think about the request.

Maintain an eye contact with the person once you have said no.

Tell John a short reason why you aren't going to do so.

Remember, once you respond by saying no. You may upset the individual. So, try to be gentle. Don't overreact.

This is the reason why you should make gum your new friend

Stressed? Overwhelmed with anxiety? Research recommends chewing a piece of chewing gum. And not only does it get rid of stress, but research shows that chewing gum intensifies the flow of blood to the brain and makes a person stay alert. Well, that is something to cheer or chew.

For many years, human beings have been searching for something to chew. The ancient Mayans and Greeks relied on tree resin, while the first "chewing gum" was created in the 1800s from chicle. Although today's gum tastes much better, the ancient Mayans and Greeks could have been searching for something. The studies indicate that the early chewers might have experienced less stress compared to those who did not chew gum.

Chewing gum is related to reduced anxiety and decreased levels of cortisol. The stress relief can happen immediately but has a long-term effect also. In one particular study, participants who were tasked to chew gum twice a day for fourteen days ranked their anxiety to be significantly lower compared to the non-chewers. Furthermore, the gum chewers not only feel less stressed but they also become more alert. In another research, participants who chewed gum and at the same time assigned to finish memory tasks had quick response time and higher levels of attention span compared to the non-chewers.

It is correct that chewing gum helps deal with anxiety, but how does that work? It may not be the chewing of gum that does the jinx, in a particular study, people who were instructed to pretend they are chewing gum didn't experience the same effects. While it is still unknown why chewing gum helps relieve stress, it may have to do with the flavor. Research recommends that flavored gum increases brain arousal as opposed to the standard gum. Chewing of gum can further activate the senses because of the smell, touch, and taste, which might explain why it has been found to improve mood and increase the level of alertness.

If you want to start to chew gum as means to reduce anxiety, make sure you pick the sugar-free gum. It contains fewer calories. Plus, it has been found to help reduce teeth cavities and clean teeth.

Chapter 3:
Face Your fears, anxiety, depression, and Worry

Anxiety Disorders-Therapy

If you are a common victim of panic attacks, worries, and obsessive thoughts, you could be disturbed by anxiety disorders. However, you don't need to live with fear and anxiety. Getting some treatment might benefit you. In fact, for most people who have been found to experience anxiety disorder, therapy has been considered the most effective treatment. Therapists can train you to learn how to manage your worries and anxiety levels, and overcome your fears.

Therapy as a treatment for anxiety disorder

Research has proven that therapy is the most effective option for treating anxiety disorders. The reason for this is anxiety therapy treats more than the symptoms of the problem. Therapy can help you rediscover the hidden causes of your fears and worries; discover the best way to relax; look at situations in a different perspective, and discover better problem-solving skills. Therapy provides you the tools to deal with anxiety and trains you how to use them.

Anxiety disorders are not the same, that means therapy should be customized to your exact symptoms and diagnosis. For example, if you are found to have OCD, you will have a different type of treatment from an individual who wants a solution to anxiety. The length of the therapy will further depend on how severe the condition is. However, the majority of anxiety therapies are short-term. Different types of therapies are designed to treat different conditions related to anxiety. However, the best methods are:

- Exposure therapy
- Cognitive behavioral therapy

Each of the anxiety therapies might be used alone or integrated with other forms of therapy.

Anxiety therapy could be applied privately or in a group.

CBT for Anxiety

CBT is a popular type of therapy known for treating anxiety conditions. Studies have been done and reported CBT to be the best treatment favorable for phobias, anxiety disorder, panic disorder and many others. CBT is designed to handle negative thought patterns. It has two components involved:

Cognitive therapy assesses the way negative thoughts contribute to anxiety.

Behavior therapy assesses how an individual behaves and react in conditions that cause anxiety.

The foundation of CBT lies in the thoughts. This is because our thoughts affect how we feel and not the state which you are going through. For instance, if your friend calls you and invites you to go and attend their birthday party. Here are some of the possible ways that you can think about the birthday invitation.

Thought#1: The party looks fun. I like to go out and make new friends.

Emotions: Excited, happy.

Thought#2: Parties are never something I enjoy going to. I'd rather stay in doors and watch some comedy.

Emotions: Neutral.

Thought#3: I don't know what to do and say at parties. I will look dejected if I go.

Emotions: Sad, anxious.

The above example shows that the same event can result in different emotions among different people. It takes us back to our expectations, attitudes, and beliefs. For the individuals who experience negative thinking, anxiety disorder, all stimulate the destructive emotions of anxiety and fear. The end goal of CBT for anxiety is to recognize and rectify these negative beliefs and thoughts. The slogan is that if you can find a way to change your mode of thinking, then it is possible to change how you feel.

Chapter 3: Face Your fears, anxiety, depression, and Worry

CBT for Challenging your thoughts and Anxiety

Thought challenging refers to the ways in which you can change the negative thinking patterns which cause anxiety. You replace them with more realistic and positive thoughts. It has three steps:

1. **Recognize the negative thoughts.** When you have an anxiety disorder, situations are seen to be more dangerous than they are.

2. **Test your negative thoughts.** Here, your therapist will help you measure the level of anxiety-triggering beliefs. This involves questioning the evidence and assessing the truth of your negative expectations. Some of the methods which you can borrow and apply in this process include weighing the pros and cons and analyzing the alternatives of what you are anxious about happening.

3. **Substitute negative thoughts with convincing thoughts.** Once you have identified irrational predictions, it is now

time to override them with new positive beliefs. Your therapist can further offer assistance in the way you build realistic statements about yourself.

To better develop a clear picture on how thought challenging operates in CBT, here is an example: Joyce can't pass close to the passageway because she's terrified she will fall, and then everyone would assume she's wild. Joyce's therapist has asked her to list down negative beliefs, highlight the gaps in her way of thinking and create a rational explanation. Below are the results.

Negative thought 1: If it happens that I collapse while on the passageway.

Cognitive alteration: The worst prediction

A truthful thought: I have never fainted, so it's rare that I may pass out on the passageway.

Negative thought 2: If I am going to pass out, it will be disgusting.

Cognitive distortion: Blowing things beyond the limit

A realistic thought: If I faint; I will recover in a few minutes. That will not be disgusting.

Negative thought 3: People are going to look at me as a crazy person.

Cognitive distortion: Jumped to a conclusion.

A realistic thought: People are going to be concerned whether I am fine.

Switching negative thoughts with accurate ones might look like something easy to do, however, it is still difficult. Why? Negative thoughts originate from a long-term thinking pattern. It requires enough practice to break this habit. That's why CBT also has personal practice. CBT can also include:

Learning to notice when you're feeling anxious and how that feels in the body.

Learning some coping skills and techniques to relax to help you overcome panic and anxiety.

Resisting your worries in practical life

Exposure therapy-anxiety

Anxiety is not a great feeling; therefore, you should avoid it if you can. A common practice which many people adopt is evading the situations which make them appear anxious. If you are petrified by tall heights, you could decide to change your route so that you don't pass near a tall height. Or if you don't like giving a public speech. Let's say that giving a public speech makes you shiver; you might decide to speak to one of your friends who is familiar or loves giving a public speech to go speak on your behalf.

However, this approach of avoiding meeting your real fear creates so much inconvenience. Besides, you will never get the right chance to fight your fears. In fact, evading your fears strengthens them.

Exposure therapy brings you face to face with the objects or situations you fear. The unique idea behind exposure therapy is that it makes you interact several times with your fears to the point where you gain total control over them. You attain a point of no more anxiety. The exposure is achieved in either one or two ways. A therapist will ask you to imagine dreadful states or you could simply interact with them in reality. With exposure therapy, you can integrate it with CBT or use it alone.

Systematic desensitization

Rather than meeting your terrifying situation immediately, systematic desensitization will allow you to slowly question your fears, cultivate confidence, and learn the skills for controlling panic. This approach has three parts:

Mastering the relaxation skills. In this part, the therapist guides you through several techniques like relaxing your muscles and taking a deep breath. You will then perform it in therapy and when you're at home on your own. Now, when you start to learn how to overcome your fears, you will frequently use the above learned techniques to reduce your anxiety response.

Listing your fears. Next, you will develop a list of 10-20 scary situations that lead to your final goal. For instance, if your ultimate goal is to conquer the fear of snakes, you can begin by looking at snake photos and then visiting a national park where there are many snakes. Each step needs to be specific, with a measurable and clear objective.

Follow the steps: By following each instruction given to you by your therapist. You can slowly begin to attempt each of the things you have listed on the list. The main thing here is to face the fearful situation until you have total control over it. This way, you'll realize that the feelings don't hurt and they vanish. Each time the anxiety becomes intense, you'll shift to the relaxation technique you have been taught. The moment you have relaxed enough; you can take back your focus to the same situation. You will need to go through the steps until you don't experience any fear.

Complementary therapies tailored for anxiety disorders

While you are busy trying to fight anxiety disorder, you could also attempt some complementary therapies designed to help reduce stress levels and allow you to attain the correct emotional balance.

Exercise. It is a natural anxiety reliever and stress buster. Studies have shown that 30 minutes of exercise 3-5 times a week can significantly relieve anxiety. To realize the required benefits, it is important to set aside one hour to perform aerobic exercise.

Relaxation methods such as mindfulness, meditation, when done every day, will help heal anxiety and boost the emotional well-being of an individual.

Biofeedback. This comes with inbuilt sensors which help monitor physiological functions like breathing rate, heart rate, and muscle tension. This will help an individual to notice the anxiety response of the body and learn how to manage it by following the correct relaxation mechanisms.

Hypnosis. Sometimes it is used together with CBT for anxiety. When you are relaxing, the therapist can use several techniques to assist you in combatting your fears.

How to make anxiety therapy work?

It is hard to find a quick solution for anxiety. Combating an anxiety disorder needs time and dedication. Therapy consists of fighting your fears instead of evading them The most important thing to do is to continue with the treatment and adhere to the advice of your therapist. If you happen to feel disappointed with the rate of recovery, remember what I said at the start about therapy-it is the best treatment for anxiety. Remain patient. You will see the benefits if you stick to them to the end.

You can still treat your anxiety problems by remaining positive. Think positive and make positive choices. Remember that, everything you do has an impact on your anxiety. So, you need to set the pathway for success by making positive decisions. Positive decisions will improve your level of relaxation.

Chapter 3: Face Your fears, anxiety, depression, and Worry

Try to study about anxiety. Combating anxiety requires many external factors. You can't just sit and wait to fight anxiety if you are not ready to find out more about your problem. Education is a key factor. While it may not treat anxiety, by virtue of you reading a few articles here and there you gain the positive feeling that anxiety can be cured.

Expand your network. Loneliness and isolation are triggering factors for anxiety. Reduce your vulnerability by meeting people. Form a habit to visit friends; join a support group; share your concerns and fears with a trusted friend.

Adopt a healthy exercise habit. Studies have shown that there is a relationship between physical activity and anxiety. This means then that you need to have time to go to the gym and work out. Don't take alcohol and stimulants as a means to treat your problem. That could just worsen the situation.

Reduce stress. List some of the things which you think are contributing to you feeling stressed. Figure out how you can handle it. Avoid sitting around people who will make you feel anxious, say no to extra tasks or responsibilities. Set aside time for relaxation and fun in your daily routine.

5 Sure-fire ways to combat fear and anxiety

If you discover that you are feeling more anxious. Here are some of the things you can do.

1. Breathing

Perhaps, you have read how you can make use of breathing to overcome anxiety.

This is worth reading also:

Breathing quickly and shallowly will help trigger other anxiety related symptoms. This means if you can manage your rate of breathing, you will succeed in stopping other symptoms of anxiety. When you feel anxious, this is what you should do:

- Stop everything you are doing.
- Pay attention to your breath

- Take a deep breath
- Then begin to breath out slowly

If you can giving it a try, you will discover how magical it is at overcoming anxiety. The most crucial thing is to breath out several times.

That sounds good. But, when you get anxious chances are that you may forget everything and all the good advice escapes through the window. This brings us to the next point.

2. Get ready

If you know that you are overwhelmed by fear and anxiety by some of the things you are about to do, such as a speech or anything that is making you shiver, you'll discover that even by thinking about it for a few seconds, you will start to experience anxiety. The end result of this effect is your whole body becomes more anxious. But, you will come to realize that the technique of breathing while thinking about your scariest situation helps you fight the anxiety. This gives you peace of mind when the actual event arrives.

One particular symptom of excessive fear or anxiety is to fail to think correctly. This happens because the emotional part of your brain overrides the analytical brain. But, in the present situation, we want to maintain a clear thought. And making sure that your brain is working clearly will help you to relax.

3. Use a different part of your brain

If you are overcome by fear, it can be difficult to think straight. But, if we can train our minds to make use of specific parts of the brain, it can be a wonderful solution in relaxing our emotions.

The simple way to achieve this has to do with numbers. You can rate your own fear on a scale of 1-10 where 10 is most fearful and 1 being fully relaxed. When feelings of anxiety strike you, figure out the number on the scale where you are. Are you on a 7 or 5? If you can do this, it will help fight the anxiety because it restarts the thinking brain, relieving the emotion and making you feel relaxed.

I remember when I was a student and was asked to give a public speech to over two hundred students. I felt very anxious before I opened my mouth to speak. But, knowing this technique, I was able to apply it, when my level of anxiety dropped to 2, I started to give the speech. It turned out to be an amazing speech and everybody applauded me. I was able to control my anxiety with this simple technique.

4. Control your imagination

Fear and anxiety are at their best whenever we start to think of the worst situations in life.

We imagine so that we can see the future and plan ahead. However, some people imagine only negative things. I don't mean a little bit of negative imagination is bad. No! The problem comes in when everything we imagine is negative. There is not a single positive. And this is the major problem that leads to fear and anxiety.

Some people negatively use their imagination and end up suffering from more anxiety compared to those who use it constructively. Anxious people and chronic worriers seem to exploit their imaginations to the point where upcoming events look catastrophic. No wonder their entire lives are filled with anxiety and fear.

Some people might not be aware that they are doing this. Here is a solution for you:

- Find a chair, sit and do some breathing in and out.

- Count from a specific number until your scale reads 1-2

- Allow yourself to be in the situation that is fearful, but look composed, relaxed and calm at the same time.

5. Adopt the AWARE technique

AWARE is an abbreviation which stands for:

A: Accepting the anxiety. Don't attempt to fight it.

W: Watch the anxiety. Simply watch it and when you can identify it, narrow down your level of fear and begin to breath longer on the out-breath.

A: Act normally. Just go on talking or doing what you were doing as if nothing has happened. This sends a dominant signal to your idle mind whose response is not required because nothing abnormal is taking place.

R: Repeat the highlighted steps in your mind when necessary.

E: Expect the best. One of the best feelings in life is when you discover that you can manage fear better than you thought possible.

Overcoming anxiety and fear will help you get the extra space in life to concentrate on what you want to do. It takes dedication and effort but just picture the rewards.

Chapter 4:
Mindful Acceptance

Have you ever felt anxious, stressed, or simply overwhelmed by life?

We live in a world with so many things to do. With texts and emails flying all around, you probably get stressed out every day. Fortunately, there is a wonderful habit that you can apply to help relax and appreciate life. We call it mindfulness.

Mindfulness is the process of putting all your attention on the present moment and accepting it without any question. This is an amazing place to start if you are searching for the major factor in happiness. If you can follow the correct steps, mindfulness will heal problems related to anxiety and stress. This will also help an individual to appreciate the little moments as they emerge. Living in a world where there is much madness and chaos, practicing mindfulness could present the best healing.

Practice Mindfulness

1. Allocate time and space to practice mindfulness

You want the time you allocate for mindfulness to be calm, quiet, and comforting. You will also prefer to select a time when you are unlikely to get disrupted. Find a peaceful and comfortable space that you can relax while you will be performing mindfulness. Let this space be specifically for practicing mindfulness. Not for something else. This will help notify your body any time you sit down to begin to calm down.

2. Focus on the current moment

Don't think about anything else. Allow your mind to remain in the present. Forget about the past or the future. This is the time to focus only on the present situation. Always return to concentrate on your breath and listen to the sounds near you.

3. Free yourself and don't do anything but be yourself.

You don't need to be running around all the time to get things done. There are times that your body wants to recharge for you to become productive. This is the moment that you can realize it. Let your mind enjoy this rest while you think of it as a way of living a good life in the long-term.

4. Avoid thinking of the past. Don't plan for the future. Don't stare at the time.

You know well that the past is gone. And you can't reverse the past. Well, why can't you forget about it? Or let it go? Stop thinking about anything that has already taken place. Don't even think of what is going to happen. Focus on the present moment without feeling worried about anything. Don't be worried about time or a task that you haven't completed.

5. Focus on your thoughts, actions, words, and motivations.

When you begin to think, say or do something, ask yourself what is the premise behind it?

6. Recognize your judgements and let them go.

It is fine to have judgements. This is something normal that everyone goes through. However, it crucial to understand them and let them disappear. Judgements are never permanent, and there is time for your mind to change, so don't get obsessed about your previous judgments.

7. Return to the present moment

If the feelings of anxiousness begin to come or you start to regret a mistake you made in the past, shift your attention back to the present moment. Tell yourself that you have no power to change anything. If it has happened, you can't reverse it.

8. Avoid being hard on yourself

Your mind will wander a bit while you are in the process of practicing mindfulness. You might begin to remember the days that you were a young boy, or even how you used to enjoy going to school while you were young. It is normal. Everyone's mind wanders a bit while they are practicing mindful meditation. So don't be too hard on yourself. Let that passing thought vanish, take a long breath and reset your focus.

Chapter 4: Mindful Acceptance

How to practice Mindfulness Meditation?

Mindfulness and meditation come with different benefits which are both mental and physical. However, most people don't recognize that the two are different things. Mindfulness is just one form of meditation.

Most people think that meditation has an instant effect, they have this belief that something is supposed to happen immediately. Some think that mediation will empty their minds and allow them to stay at peace in a split second. Others think that they should feel weightless.

Meditation and mindfulness, what is the difference?

To clear the doubt, mindfulness involves being alert. You can practice mindfulness at any time of the day. For example, you can practice it while having a small talk with your close relative.

Mindfulness meditation refers to a well-known type of meditation among the Buddhists. If you are interested in integrating the two into a single mindful meditation, here are the steps.

1. Allocate time to practice

No need to have a fixed time. But, if you can set something to alert you like an alarm or even develop a certain habit, it will trigger your body to assume the state of meditation.

2. Find a place which is free of disturbances

It could be a room where nobody passes or comes in. As long as you ensure that the place is silent and has no interruptions.

3. Relax yourself

Get a position which will allow you to feel comfortable. It can be a seat or a mat. Remember, sitting down while meditating is the best way to go. You can decide to sit, stand or kneel. The choice is up to you to decide. But, make sure that you don't have tight clothes on which can prevent you from breathing freely.

4. Now, concentrate on the movements of your legs

5. Sit straight, but remain relaxed

Let your backbone take its normal curve. Comfort is very important here.

6. Your arms should be loose

Now, loose your hands while you bend your elbow slowly. Your upper arms should be in parallel with your upper body; and place your palms whenever it feels comfortable.

7. Relax your gaze

Let your chin go down and permit your eyelids to move downward. No need to close your eyes. Just stare at anything that crosses your eyes.

8. Relax your whole body

You can begin with your toes until you are completely relaxed with the whole body. But, don't forget your shoulders, jaw, face etc.

9. Spend some time to think about your intention.

This should not take long. Start with simple details for performing mindfulness, and your defined goals. You might want to feel energized for the entire day, or you might aim to reduce the amount of judgement which bothers you often on a regular basis.

10. Pay attention to your breath

Take some 8-20 seconds to think about the air which you breathe in, how it flows through your breathing system. Think about the good feeling you experience when you breath in and breath out.

11. Recognize when your mind starts to wander

This is fine, but you don't want to force away any passive beliefs. When you find your mind starting to wander, slowly return it to breathing.

12. Excuse your wandering mind

Sometimes, your mind might begin to wander every now and then. In this case, don't fight it. Just stop and watch it as it wanders.

13. When you are through, raise your gaze gently

Just remember, meditation has no perfect time. You can meditate in the morning, afternoon or

3. Practice abdominal breathing

Breath like you are directing all the air into your stomach. If you breath out, do so through your mouth gently and allow your stomach to return back to its normal position.

4. Know the difference between deep and shallow breathing

Shallow breathing will stop at the chest but abdominal breathing takes over your entire lungs. Plus, it will facilitate complete oxygen exchange.

Mindfulness is good if you aim at relieving your cognitive symptoms of depression. By concentrating in the present moment, it helps many individuals to recognize their negative thoughts. They also recognize that the negative thoughts exist without making any judgement, and they realize that those thoughts don't depict the reality. Furthermore, mindfulness will help individuals to discover their thoughts aren't that powerful and allow them to vanish fast.

If one can learn and understand the way they think rather than getting carried away by emotions of their own thoughts, it becomes very hard for them to be dragged down by any negative thinking. You develop total control of your thoughts. This way, when the thoughts come, you are able to manage them.

It is also good to develop a connection with mother nature when you are trying to fight depression. Set aside some time to bask in the sunshine, it can have a big impact on one's physical and mental well-being.

Nature is the best boost for your mental well-being. If you go to work in an office, spend a few moments to stare at nature. It will help boost your overall well-being. Notice and accept the situation when you feel scared or depressed. Think about how active your stress response is instead of how inadequate you are as an individual.

Practice writing a gratitude journal every night. Building a culture of gratitude is free, and it doesn't take a lot of time, but there is a possibility you'll get massive benefits from it.

The benefits of practicing mindfulness

The benefits of mindfulness and meditation are widely known in the scientific community. Here are some of the positive effects one gets by practicing mindfulness:

- **Reduction of stress.** Practicing mindfulness has proven to reduce the amount of cortisol in our bodies. Besides lowering our stress in the present, it also helps us reduce stress in the long-term and in response to future events.

- **More creativity**. Innovation and thinking creatively take place in the neocortex of the brain. For the neocortex to function correctly, we have to clear our mind of emotional thoughts. Mindfulness is the perfect medicine for doing this.

- **Improved health**. There are specific studies which have proven mindfulness can heal someone and increase emotional intelligence. Mindfulness makes people become compassionate.

- **Fights depression**.

The bottom line

Meditation is an amazing medicine for anxiety.

It goes beyond temporarily helping you relax. It goes into a deep level by changing the structure and function of your brain. Meditation reprograms your brain so that it becomes less anxious. Mindfulness meditation needs no special training and can bring anxiety relief in just 10 minutes a day.

Learning how to quiet your mind can be very challenging, however, guided meditation makes everything easy. It gives you the chance to apply knowledge and techniques from the best meditation experts.

Chapter 5:
Narrowing down your specific Worries

Containing your Worry

Even though a little bit of worry is normal is the way every one of us was created, there are times when it can feel like we are worrying too much. Containing your worry is all about letting yourself worry no matter what happens, but only at the designated time of the day which you decide yourself.

The first thing you need to turn your focus to when containing your worry is uncertainty. This is the most common types of worry which a lot of people experience right from when you are a child. You are worried about what you are going to eat tomorrow. Some people are worried about how they are going to arrive at their places of work. If you realize that you are worrying about something whose end result is uncertain, soon you will start feeling overwhelmed that you have no control over the situation. And this can have a negative impact on the rest of your life. Most of these worries begin with what if...?

Alternatively, there are some things which we worry about but we don't know that we can solve them here and now. So, when we narrow down the worries, we look at practical worries which you have the ability to deal with and hypothetical worries which depend on uncertainty.

Face your Career Crisis and Financial Woes

Many people worry a lot about money. They are obsessed about their savings, home values, accounts, and promotions. More basic needs add a lot of worry. People are worriesd about losing their job, and the ability to provide the basic needs like clothing, shelter, and healthcare. Even though money is not more worthy than a person, we all need some amount of money to live.

Dealing with job anxieties

Nearly everyone is always worried about losing their job. You are not the only one. Even CEOs of top companies are always worried about the future of their company. An economic recession is something that will happen without any notice. It occurs spontaneously, and the results are catastrophic because millions of people can lose their jobs. It is very difficult to be sure whether a given career will continue to exist or it will be phased out. For example, there was a time when if you worked in a car manufacturing company, your job was considered safe.

These days, technology has been good and bad. It has increased the number of jobs in some sectors while reducing jobs in other sectors.

Change the look of your resume

One of best ways that you can be sure to handle anxiety related to jobs is to make use of the market opportunities. Whether you already have a job or you have just landed your first job, having a good resume is a must. If you don't know how to make your resume nice, you can hire a professional resume writer who can help create an attractive resume for you.

I know someone might be asking, why should I hire a professional resume writer? Well, if you didn't know, updating a resume is not something easy, I have seen a lot of people feel anxious when they want to update or edit their resume. And don't forget that when you are anxious, most people evade doing that particular thing which makes them feel anxious. Now, this is the reason why I recommend that you look for a professional resume writing company to help you. Below are more suggestions which you can use:

- Develop a schedule of how you want to update your resume. Your schedule should be specific on what you want to achieve.

- After you have updated your resume, present it to your friends to give you some feedback about it.

- Don't procrastinate about anything. Procrastinating will only increase your level of anxiety.

Make sure that your resume is short and highlights your strengths in the best possible way. Include keywords in your resume. The keywords should be related to the job you are looking for.

Developing flexibility

It does not matter what you are going through or what you have gone through. It could be that you have lost your job today, or they have transferred you to a different department. As long as you are a flexible person, you will still overcome all the challenges which you encounter on the way. One of the unique things about people who are flexible is their ability to deal with the challenges that come on their way. Because they are highly flexible, they don't give up but adjust their situations in accordance with the challenges.

I am talking about people who today are discontinued from their job, but in the next minute, they are already applying for new jobs. Flexibility is key to realizing success and overcoming some of the stress related to jobs.

While people who are not flexible will feel angry and frustrated. Flexible people appreciate the situation and figure out their next strategy. Inflexible people will remain adamant about change and resist making changes to their previous choices, but this is not the same with flexible people. They always try something new, they are driven by the passion to achieve something different.

When you have this mental flexibility, you are strong enough to handle all the difficulties which you go through. You will know when to back off and when it is right to create a balance. Having a mental flexibility gives you the freedom to look at reality from a different angle.

A person with mental flexibility will understand that when change comes it is inevitable. This level of flexibility needs someone to be open to new experiences. One must know that truth is hard to tell.

Stable career

While people live an anxious life, it is understood that if your career is stable, you will not worry too much. One of the best things about ensuring that you don't worry so much is to develop a mechanism for handling the future. If you can increase your level of education. It is well and good. Education improves your level of knowledge and skills. This will make you a better person.

However, you need to also know that every career has its own problems. No career is stable. You could be laughing now, and then tomorrow crying.

Maintain your focus

If you are vulnerable to fear and anxiety, you will forever be controlled by fear. I say this because most people who are about to lose their jobs begin to think about so many negative things in their lives. These negative thoughts then ruin their lives.

I will suggest that if you are working, it is important to develop a culture of saving part of your income. If you can cultivate this culture. I am sure you will help reduce some of the fears and worries that you go through when you lose your job. Another thing which you need to do is to cut down on your expenses. If you can reduce your expenses, you will help save some income.

Dedicate yourself to a new strategy

If you can design a new strategy to use, it can help you stop worrying about your jobs and money. Can you imagine if you have a passive stream of income which at the end of every month you make a massive income? In this case, you know that even if you are going to lose your job, you will still manage to pay your monthly bills. And this gives you peace of mind.

Planning for the future

A few years ago, people used to work for over 40 years in a single company and look forward to living a better life later when they retire. Today, everything has changed. Pension plans have gone high.

While you may be right to be worried about not being able to enjoy your retirement years. If you can make use of the flexibility trait, you will be in a better state than that person who does not learn to be flexible. By being flexible, you will learn to handle the future while remaining composed. You will not be overwhelmed with fear or anxiety. By realizing that uncertainty has

Chapter 5: Narrowing down your specific Worries

limits, you will begin to adapt to the different ways in which you can handle it.

Chapter 6:
Blue Print for Well-being

Transform the way you think and your attitude

At times, a lot of stress can lead to a thousand thoughts which are triggered by a little problem. But, the results are devastating. We get worked up sometime, and this irrational thought can lead to undue stress. However, with cognitive restructuring, you get to learn how you can control these kinds of thoughts and remain positive and realistic.

Cognitive restructuring is a behavioral technique related to cognitive therapy. This consists of learning how to change your way of thinking. Transform the wrong style of thinking and develop positive thinking.

How it works

There is nothing so frustrating than getting caught in a traffic jam while heading to work. Like many people, you perhaps get irritated, frustrated and angry. You might start to be worried about getting to work late or even failing to meet the deadlines of the day's tasks. These thoughts then give birth to stress.

You now have two choices: To let the stress destroy you until you lose your job or transform your way of thinking.

Cognitive restructuring focuses on thoughts, identifies when the thoughts are irrational, and lets you learn how to replace the thoughts and behaviors. Taking the example of the traffic scenario, think about rational situations. Does that situation lead you to feel stressed? Remember, this is a situation in which there's nothing that you can do to help you arrive early at your job. You can't step out of the vehicle and walk to your destination. It is, therefore, irrational to begin to imagine terrible things that might never happen. Rather than imagining those negative scenarios, focus your energy on the way you can evade getting caught in traffic the next time and stay away from stress.

This is how you can change your thoughts

Start by evaluating your fears and thoughts and find out whether they are rational or irrational.

You can ask yourself the following questions about your fears and thoughts.

- What is the worst possible result for this scenario?

- Can it harm me or any of my family?

- Am I assessing this situation in the right way and what proof do I have for my fears

- What effort or step can I do to change the situation

Begin by writing down on a sheet of paper your thoughts and highlight some of the facts that you know. Re-evaluate the facts, and create a comparison with your fears and thoughts, and figure out which one is rational.

It is possible to change your own thinking habits by yourself, but not many people can do that. Some people have the ability to learn new ways of thinking with the help of their processing ability and observation skills. For some, it does not occur quickly and they may need the help of a good therapist.

Develop a strong personal control

The weight on personal control is enormous. People who are not affected by depression or stress direct their energy to matters over which they have control but not things which are beyond their, limits.

Break bad habits

Fear can drive us to the point where we recognize and recall all our negative thoughts, this then makes us create the image in our mind where we view the world as a terrifying place to live. However, we can put an end to this trend by deliberately identifying the positive aspects and feeling joy we experience when we get in touch with someone who we love.

According to research done by Barbara Fredrickson it was discovered that positivity broadens our perspective. We have a wider view that gives us more options. And the more times we apply positivity, the more it builds, developing a resilience which permits us to function even in the hard times.

Get support

Fear can make us feel disconnected from the rest of our close friends. Finding support could be the best thing to help you become your normal self. Having friends and family members stay close to us can help us develop a sense of security. When we feel secure we become confident to deal with other related issues in life.

Different ways to help you come out of your fears

We all experience fears, anxieties and phobias. Sometimes we close our eyes and hold our breath while we ride the elevator to the 12th floor of an office building, while others just avoid going to the funeral because of the fear of seeing a coffin. Well, here are four different strategies which you can apply.

1. Focus on what is right before you

This is true of many things. If we can maintain our focus on what is right before our eyes, we have good chance to remain relaxed. This applies also when you find yourself in the midst of a stressful scenario.

2. Keep your cheerleaders close

Overcoming your fears is simple when you are in the company of your cheerleaders or friends. This is true whether you decide to challenge yourself to run a marathon or give a public speech.

3. Pay attention to your breath

Breathe in and breathe out but make sure that breathing out takes longer than breathing in. When you breathe in deeply, you activate your vagus nerve, which runs from your medulla oblongata situated in the brain stem, to the stomach. The long nerve connects the main nervous coordination and your central nervous system. It is often considered the link between our conscious and subconscious minds.

4. Apply some humor

Some jokes can help you feel relaxed and control the situation.

In summary, to face your fears and anxieties you need to stand strong. Identify some of the ways of developing personal control in your life.

1. Practice stress reduction mechanism like mindfulness.

2. Shift your focus to the positive emotions in your daily life.

3. Work and identify meaning in your life

4. Get support from your friends.

Still, if you are threatened by fear, don't forget other areas of your life.

Conclusion

Thank for making it through to the end of this book, let's hope it was informative and able to provide you with all of the tools you need to achieve your goals whatever they may be.

Sometimes change can be terrifying. The lack of control and anxiety involved can be confusing and frustrating to everyone. We all need support from our friends and families at certain point in our lives, often when we are in the process of learning something new or changing circumstances that we are in.

Most of the things which we learn in life are terrifying; including learning how to drive a car, learn how to ride a bike, etc. Take, for instance, mastering how to swim. Many young adults and children are afraid of getting into the water. However, given the right instruction, support and guidance we can develop ways to overcome our fears and master the different stages involved. Similarly, panic disorder, anxiety, phobias, and depression are no different.

Cognitive Behavioral Therapy

If we can understand why we behave and believe the way we do, there are a lot of things which we can do that will help:

- To change those behaviors and beliefs

- Develop correct, positive feelings about our self.

- Develop the correct feelings of being confident and in control

Once we recognize that courage is not the lack of fear we are in a position to go forward. Some guidance and support is helpful, but there are times when it is very frightening. If we want to grow and become better individuals, we shouldn't let fear hold us back.

We might feel that our problem is unique and it needs specific help. Yet similar experiences lie at the heart of all these problems. They grow and expand in the same way and we are weakened in the same way.

28318612R10111

Printed in Great Britain
by Amazon